THE
MORRIS CERULLO
FINANCIAL PLANNER

But remember the LORD your God, for it is
he who gives you the ability to produce
wealth, and so confirms his covenant, which
he swore to your forefathers, as it is today.

Deuteronomy 8:18, NIV

MORRIS CERULLO WORLD EVANGELISM

U.S.: P.O. Box 85277 • San Diego, CA 92186-5277
Canada: P.O. Box 3600 • Concord, Ontario L4K1B6
U.K.:P.O. Box 277 • Hemel Hempstead, HERTS HP2 7DH

THE MORRIS CERULLO

FINANCIAL PLANNER

TABLE OF CONTENTS

THIS IS YOUR HOUR FOR FINANCIAL FREEDOM

With all my heart I believe that this is the hour for God's people to break through the financial bondage in their lives. God is releasing His power and a financial anointing to enable you to break free of every debt and financial problem.

The purpose of this financial planner is to enable you to develop a Life/Financial plan that is focused upon fulfilling God's purpose for your life. God does not want you to be limited by your current financial circumstances.

You may be so far in debt that you do not know how it will ever be possible to be completely debt-free. You may be struggling with long-standing financial problems and do not know what to do. Or, you may be out of debt but do not understand God's plan to prosper you.

So often when people do their financial planning, they plan according to their current financial limitations. God wants to take you beyond these limitations to a new spiritual dimension whereby you believe Him for those things that may seem impossible to you. He wants to open your spiritual eyes to see His unlimited resources that He is waiting to release into your life…the things you have been waiting for…the things He has revealed that are part of His plan for your life and ministry. You have been unable to take hold of these blessings because your eyes have been focused upon your own limited natural resources.

But today is your day to break free of debt and begin a new journey of living in the supernatural provision of God!

You do not need to hear more of man's theology or more head-knowledge. You need to hear, "Thus saith the Lord"…what God's Word reveals, and what God is saying to you in this end-time hour concerning your finances!

As God's plan of supernatural provision is unveiled to you through His Word, you will have a new understanding of the covenant relationship God entered into with you. You will no longer depend upon your own limited natural resources. You will receive a financial breakthrough in which you will live in a **cycle** where you experience His supernatural provision in your life.

A "cycle" is a period of time in which an event takes place. This is a period of time for a great financial shaking…and the event to take place in this cycle

is the release of your end-time financial anointing!

God has revealed His plan concerning His supernatural provision. Look carefully at the following verses:

> *"And God is able to make all grace (every favor and earthly blessing) come to you in abundance, so that you may always and under all circumstances and whatever the need, be self-sufficient-possessing enough to require no aid or support and furnished in abundance for every good work and charitable donation…And God who provides seed to the sower and bread for eating will also provide and multiply your [resources for] sowing, and increase the fruits of your righteousness [which manifests itself in active goodness, kindness and charity]. Thus you will be enriched in all things and in every way, so that you can be generous, [and your generosity as it is] administered by us will bring forth thanksgiving to God."*
>
> *2 Corinthians 9:8, 10-11, AMP*

Does this sound like God intends you to go lacking or that you will barely survive? NO! He planned not only for your needs to be met but that you will have an abundance so that you will be able to give generously to fulfill His will in this end-time hour!

You will be "enriched in all things and in every way." He said God will "provide and multiply your resources for sowing!"

In these verses, there are three powerful keys to walking in financial victory and living in God's cycle of supernatural provision:

1. God will provide seed for you to sow.

2. God will supply your need.

3. God will multiply your seed

Look at this illustration of God's cycle of supernatural provision:

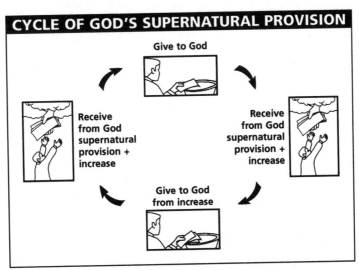

It never fails...it is self-perpetuating because it is God's Supply.

Not only do you reap a yield from the initial seed that you sow, but also the **increase** of the seed sown. As a result, you reap many times over and above what you plant. From this abundance, you have sufficient supply for your needs and **more** to sow back into the Kingdom of God.

You need not struggle to produce the seed, it is God Who PROVIDES ABUNDANTLY the seed for you to sow. As you plant a seed, God takes what you give and MULTIPLIES it until there is an ABUNDANCE. Then, as you take part of your harvest and sow it back into the work of God, He multiplies it again.

The more you give to God and to the work of building the Kingdom of God, the more you will RECEIVE in return...the more you will be able to GIVE...the more you will RECEIVE...until you live in a cycle of God's Supernatural Provision in which there is a **continual** flow of God's blessing and provision in your life.

My prayer is that as you use this financial planner and apply the truths from God's Word concerning His desire to bless and prosper you, you will live continually in this cycle of God's supernatural provision!

Morris Cerullo

RELINQUISH OWNERSHIP OF ALL THAT YOU HAVE TO GOD

He that findeth his life shall lose it: and he that loseth his life for my sake shall find it.

Matthew 10:39

And Jesus answered and said, Verily I say unto you, There is no man that hath left house, or brethren, or sisters, or father, or mother, or wife, or children or lands, for my sake and the gospel's. But he shall receive an hundredfold now in this time, houses, and brethren, and sisters, and mothers, and children, and lands, with persecutions; and in the world to come eternal life.

Mark 10:29-30

SECTION 1
RELINQUISH OWNERSHIP OF ALL THAT YOU HAVE TO GOD

Financial planning must begin with a personal evaluation, not only of your current financial profile, but also with your attitude toward money, your knowledge concerning God's principles about money and His plan of provision for your life. Your attitude concerning money will affect all your decisions about what you do with it.

If you do not have a clear understanding concerning what God's Word teaches about money and know His promises to you, you will be unable to follow His plan and walk in His supernatural provision.

Your finances are important to God!

How you spend your money is important to Him!

To live in God's cycle of supernatural provision you cannot rely upon your natural mind in developing your financial plan. The Apostle Paul said, *"For to be carnally minded is death; but to be spiritually minded is life and peace. Because the carnal mind is enmity against God: for it is not subject to the law of God, neither indeed can be." (Romans 8:6-7)* This is why it is so important that your mind first be renewed by the Word before you develop your financial plan. You cannot rely upon your natural mind or man's limited understanding. You must base all your actions upon God's Word.

In this first section you will learn important spiritual principles based upon God's Word that you will be able to use and apply in the practical areas of your finances.

The Apostle Paul said, *"And be constantly renewed in the spirit of your mind – having a fresh mental and spiritual attitude;" (Ephesians 4:23, AMP)*

He told the Romans, *"Do not be conformed to the world – this age, fashioned after and adapted to its external, superficial customs. Be transformed (changed) by the (entire) renewal of your mind – by its new ideals and its new attitude – so that you may prove (for yourselves) what is the good and acceptable and perfect will of God, even the thing which is good and acceptable and perfect (in His sight for you)." (Romans 12:2, AMP)*

THE MORRIS CERULLO FINANCIAL PLANNER

You cannot afford to follow the world's methods or principles concerning money and finances. A spirit of greed and selfishness has taken hold. The philosophy of the world today concerning success and riches is to obtain as much money, houses, land, stocks and investments as possible and store them up. This philosophy is based upon the idea that one gains through getting.

The world's perspective concerning money is:

- Get as much as you can.

- Spend as much as you can while enjoying and acquiring worldly possessions.

- Store up as much as you can for the future.

The Kingdom perspective concerning money is:

- God is the source of all your money and finances.

- Give your money freely and liberally to God as He directs.

- Do not store up worldly riches, but rather store up treasures in heaven.

ALL YOUR FINANCES AND POSSESSIONS BELONG TO GOD

The attitude of the vast majority of people today concerning their money is that all they have acquired is because of their hard work and it belongs to them to do with as they please.

The Kingdom perspective is that everything we own God has given to us. All our money and possessions actually belong to the Lord. God has made us stewards and we are accountable to Him for the way we use the assets He has given us.

You are not free to use your finances irresponsibly or without accountability. *"Now it is required that those who have been given a trust must prove faithful." (I Corinthians 4:2, NIV)* As a steward, it is important to God how you spend your money.

The focus of the majority of the people of the world regarding obtaining money and accumulating wealth and possessions is to look to their own limited abilities, paycheck, job, employer, businesses, investments and banks as their source.

The Kingdom perspective is to recognize and look to God as our Source. We must depend upon Him as our Source of Supply and trust Him for our daily provision.

THE KINGDOM PRINCIPLE IS THAT YOU GAIN THROUGH GIVING!

Jesus taught that in order for us to really live, we must be willing to give our lives away. He said, *"He that findeth his life shall lose it: and he that loseth his life for my sake shall find it." (Matthew 10:39)* Jesus said that those who cling to their own lives in this world will lose them, but those who give their lives for His sake will truly live, and inherit eternal life.

The Apostle Paul considered the loss of all things as great gain. He said, *"...I have suffered the loss of all things, and do count them but dung, that I may win Christ..." (Philippians 3:8)* Jesus said that those who are willing to give up houses, lands, wives, mothers, fathers and children for His sake will receive one-hundredfold in this life! (Luke 18:29-30).

This truth is one of the Laws of Spiritual and Financial harvest. Jesus taught:

"...Unless a grain of wheat falls into the earth and dies, it remains [just one grain; never becomes more but lives] by itself alone. But if it dies, it produces many others and yields a rich harvest."

John 12:24, AMP

A seed cannot produce anything until it is first sown into the ground and dies. The potential is there within it to produce a harvest, but it lies dormant until it is sown into the soil.

Your life is a seed you sow. Only as you are willing to give it away, by dying to self, will you gain life. Your life will not produce a harvest until you give it away. As you give your life away for Christ's sake by planting seeds of love, faithfulness, obedience and commitment into the Kingdom of God, you will reap a great harvest.

Give and you will receive!

The same principle is true regarding ownership of your finances, wealth and material possessions. Only as you are willing to transfer ownership of all that you have and all that you are to God, will God demonstrate His ability upon your behalf and release His blessings.

If you have not already done so, tell the Father right now that you willingly surrender and transfer ownership of all your money and possessions to Him. Make a commitment from this day forward that you will consistently seek God's will in all your finances and material things instead of relying upon yourself.

SEEDTIME

HEBREW – "Zera". This word refers to the process of scattering seed. In the beginning, God established a natural universal law of the harvest. Seedtime and Harvest is a perpetual process of sowing and reaping. As long as the earth remains there will be seedtime, a time of sowing seeds into the ground to produce a harvest. The seed possesses within itself the ability to multiply and produce other seeds. Each seed produces after its own species. An apple seed produces an apple tree, corn seed produces stalks of corn, and wheat seed produces wheat. The size of the harvest is determined by the amount and type of seed sown at seedtime.

In the spiritual realm, there is also "seedtime"…a time when an individual sows seeds that will produce a harvest in his life. The seeds we sow are things which we give. There is "good seed" and "bad seed". Time, natural abilities, love, acts of kindness, faith, are all "good seed". Unbelief, selfishness, fear, bitterness, hatred, cruelty are all "bad seed". In the financial harvest, the seeds we sow are the gifts and offerings we give to God. The seed contains the potential to multiply and produce a harvest, but until we sow…give to God the very best of what we have…we cannot expect to reap a harvest.

RELINQUISH OWNERSHIP OF ALL THAT YOU HAVE TO GOD

WORKSHEET

Your attitude concerning money will affect all your decisions about what you do with it. Your money represents you. It represents your time, talents, abilities and your hard work.

Evaluate your attitude toward money and your material possessions by answering the following questions. Ask God to reveal any areas where your attitude regarding money needs to change and your mind renewed by His Word:

a. Do I consider that everything I own (money, time, talent, abilities and possessions) belongs to God and consistently seek his will first before making decisions regarding my finances? Circle one.
❑ Always ❑ Often ❑ Occasionally ❑ Never

b. You cannot serve God and money. How much of my time, talents, energy and abilities am I spending in an attempt to acquire more money? Circle one.
❑ 25% ❑ 50% ❑ 75% ❑ 100%

c. Am I placing my desire to acquire more money and worldly possessions above my desire for God and doing His will?

❑ Yes ❑ No

Jesus said: "No one can serve two masters; for either he will hate the one and love the other, or he will stand by and be devoted to the one and despise and be against the other. You cannot serve God and mammon [that is, deceitful riches, money, possessions or what is trusted in].
Matthew 6:24, AMP

---

d. Am I content with having my basic necessities and the needs of my family met, or am I continually striving to obtain more money and worldly possessions?

❑ Yes, I have learned to be content with having my basic needs met.

❑ No, I am continually striving to acquire more of the world's wealth and possessions for my own needs and desires.

In this materialistic society, we should not strive to acquire more money or worldly possessions. Read 1 Timothy 6:6-10. In these verses, the Apostle Paul states that godliness with contentment is "great gain." Then, he defines contentment as being satisfied with the very basics of having food and clothing. *"And having food and raiment let us be therewith content." (1 Timothy 6:8).*

Paul said, *"For the love of money is the root of all evil..." (verse 10)* He did not say "money is the root of all evil". He said *"...the love of money is the root..."* In the New American Standard version, this is translated, *"For the love of money is a root of all sorts of evil..." (1 Timothy 6:10, NAS)*

The evil that Paul pointed out in this verse is covetousness, which is a greedy desire and continual grasping for money that leads men away from their faith.

Money is not evil. The sin is coveting after money and trusting in riches. The spirit of covetousness and the spirit of mammon often gain control and become the driving forces in peoples' lives, which brings corruption and leads to destruction.

Money can be the means of a blessing or cursing in your life. If you use it wisely and are liberal in your giving to God and ministering to the needs of others, you will be blessed. However, if you begin to love your money so much that you are not liberal in your giving to God and hoard it for yourself or use it only for selfish reasons, you will bring sorrow upon yourself. Solomon wrote, *"There is a sore evil which I have seen under the sun, namely, riches kept for the owners thereof to their hurt." (Ecclesiastes 5:13)*

As you review your finances and develop your financial plan, make it one of your goals to learn to be content, as the Apostle Paul did, with having your basic needs met. Instill this principle within your family

1. What is God's purpose for money He gives me? (Check the answers that you believe are the most accurate.)

❑ To meet all my needs.

❑ To store it up for myself.

❑ To enable me to acquire more worldly possessions.

❑ To enable me to minister to the needs of others.

❑ To enable me to help finance the end-time harvest of souls and fulfill the great commission.

We hear a lot of preaching and teaching regarding how God will bless and prosper us as we give to Him. We know that our God will supply our needs. We know that as we faithfully give our tithes and offerings God will open the windows of heaven and pour out such a blessing upon us that we will not even be able to contain it! As we give according to His Word, we can stand in faith and claim these promises.

However, God's purpose for releasing His promised blessings in our lives is not just so we can acquire an abundance of the world's wealth for our own personal use. God does not intend to multiply His blessings back into our lives so that we can acquire more worldly possessions.

God's purpose for prospering His people is not only to meet our needs, but to fulfill the work in bringing in the final harvest. It will take a tremendous amount of money to finance the end-time harvest of souls. The world will not finance it; it is up to God's people.

The money that God gives you is a means of winning souls!

Your money is a means of training Nationals!

Your money is a means of providing the ministry tools for national evangelists to reach their nations with the Gospel!

Guard against the "Bless me" mentality that has become so prevalent within the Church and causes people to be more concerned about the blessings they expect to receive than using their money to fulfill God's will. Consecrate your money and set it aside for the purpose God intended. Ask God to release the flow of His blessings upon your finances and make you one of His end-time financiers!

2. Looking back over your last year's major expenditures, ask yourself, "Did I seek God's wisdom and direction regarding how to use my money?"

❏ Yes ❏ No

3. Do I own my money and possessions or do they own me?

Read Mark 10:17-27.

In this story, a young man who believed in Jesus and was eager to know how to inherit eternal life, came running after Jesus and fell at His feet. *"Good Master, what shall I do that I may inherit eternal life?" (verse 17)*

Jesus answered, "You know the commandments: 'Do not murder, do not commit adultery, do not steal, do not give false testimony, do not defraud, honor your father and mother." (Mark 10:19, NIV)

The young man answered that he had kept all these commandments from his youth. He had lived a good moral life and had kept all the commandments. Yet, he was still hungry for more of God and was ready to do whatever necessary to inherit eternal life.

Jesus looked upon the young man, saw his intense desire and love for God, and loved him. However, He saw deep into the innermost recesses of his heart and knew that the young man was trusting in his riches.

Imagine the look on the young man's face as Jesus looked deep into his eyes and said, "One thing you lack…Go, sell everything you have and give to the poor, and you will have treasure in heaven. Then come, follow me." (Mark 10:21, NIV) When the young man heard this, I imagine his heart was grieved, he hung his head, rose to his feet and sadly walked away. One thing was lacking in this young man's life that stopped him from following Jesus. His possessions had such a hold on him that he was unwilling to give them up to follow Jesus. He lost his opportunity and went away grieved because he could not give up his possessions.

It was not the riches he possessed that held the young ruler back from following Jesus. It was his love and trust in them and the security they provided.

If Jesus were to look deep into your eyes and ask you to sell all your possessions and give the proceeds to the poor or to the work of God, would you do it? Would you be willing to cash in some of your stocks and bonds or sell property you have been holding onto as a "safety measure?"

Regardless of how much you may or may not have, it is possible to have your trust in your wealth instead of having your trust and confidence in God.

It is important for you to search deeply into your heart to determine if you, like this rich young ruler, have placed your confidence and trust in your wealth and worldly possessions. In the coming worldwide financial crisis, those who trust in their wealth will be shaken. That is why it is important for you now to have your trust and confidence in God and His supernatural provision for your life.

TRANSFER OF OWNERSHIP

DATE OF TRANSFER: _____

I, _____, HEREBY TRANSFER OWNERSHIP OF ALL MY WORLDLY GOODS AND ASSETS, INCLUDING ALL BANK AND SAVINGS ACCOUNTS, HOUSES, LANDS, STOCKS, BONDS, INVESTMENTS, CARS, FURNITURE AND ALL THAT I OWN TO ALMIGHTY GOD.

I RELINQUISH ALL CONTROL, CLAIMS AND RIGHTS TO THE AFOREMENTIONED ASSETS AND GIVE FULL CONTROL TO GOD. I RECOGNIZE THAT I AM GOD'S STEWARD AND AS HIS STEWARD, I WILL FAITHFULLY SEEK AND FOLLOW HIS DIRECTION IN HANDLING THE ASSETS HE HAS ENTRUSTED TO ME.

I HEREBY DEDICATE AND CONSECRATE ALL OF MY FUTURE EARNINGS TO GOD. IN EVERY TRANSACTION, I WILL ACT IN ACCORDANCE WITH HIS WILL.

_____
SIGNED

REMEMBER GOD AS YOUR SOURCE

*B*eware that you do not forget the Lord your God, by not keeping His commandments, His precepts, and His statutes, which I command you today. Lest when you have eaten and are full, and have built goodly houses, and live in them, And when your herds and flocks multiply, and your silver and gold is multiplied, and all you have is multiplied; Then your [mind and] heart be lifted up, and you forget your God who brought you out of the land of Egypt, out of the house of bondage…And beware lest you say in your [mind and] heart, My power and the might of my hand have gotten me this wealth.

Deuteronomy 8:11-14, 17, AMP

SECTION 1 (A)
REMEMBER GOD AS YOUR SOURCE

As you begin to develop your financial plan, listed below are six major keys to walking in the prosperity God has planned for you.

1. Know it is God's will to prosper you.

2. Know God's promises and act upon them in faith.

3. Honor God with your "substance".

4. Remember God as your source of supply.

5. Saturate your heart and mind with the Word and walk in faith and obedience to it.

6. Ask in faith, believing that you will receive.

God is the source of your wealth! David wrote, *"THE EARTH is the Lord's and the fulness thereof; the world, and they that dwell therein." (Psalm 24:1)* God said, *"The silver is mine, and the gold is mine, saith the Lord of hosts." (Haggai 2:8)* The wealth you have today is a gift from God. It is His blessing upon your life and He wants you to enjoy it. He wants you to recognize Him as the Source of your wealth and praise Him for it.

"But thou shalt remember the Lord thy God: for it is he that giveth thee power to get wealth, that he may establish his covenant which he sware unto thy fathers, as it is this day."
Deuteronomy 8:18

In these verses there is one of the most important keys to living in a cycle of God's supernatural provision: God is your Source! No one but God can give you the power to get wealth!

Your job or your employer is not your source. They are just the current resources God is using to bless you. God has unlimited resources! There is no lack in His house! When you receive a full revelation of this great truth, that

God desires to pour out His blessings and prosper you, you will be able to take hold of His promises by faith to receive all that you need.

Moses told the children of Israel to REMEMBER God's supernatural provision for them during their forty years of wandering in the wilderness. God fed them with manna to teach them that man does not live by bread alone, but by every word that comes out of the mouth of God. (Deuteronomy 8:3)

He warned them of the danger of forgetting God as their Source and of being exalted in their own eyes, thinking that it was through their own efforts that they had obtained their wealth.

Satan's strategy is to get you to forget God as your Source, to get you to rely upon your own strength and abilities instead of looking to and depending upon God for His daily provision.

When you know God is your Source of Total Supply and remember that it is He who gives you power to get wealth, you will reject the lies that Satan feeds many Christians – that they were born to be poor or that it is God's will that they are poor.

When you REMEMBER that God is your Source and will supply **all your need**, not according to man's limited abilities but according to His **unlimited resources**, you will no longer be fearful or worried about your financial problems. In the midst of great financial crisis, you will not be shaken but you will walk in victory, knowing He will abundantly supply all your needs.

GOD WANTS YOU TO ENJOY THE FRUIT OF YOUR LABOR

Not only does God give you the power to get wealth, He gives you the ability to enjoy all that He gives you. *"The blessing of the Lord, it maketh rich, and he addeth no sorrow with it." (Proverbs 10:22)*

The wealth and riches of this world often bring pain and sorrow with them. *"Whoever loves money never has money enough; whoever loves wealth is never satisfied with his income..." (Ecclesiastes 5:10, NIV)* Solomon, who was one of the richest men who ever lived also wrote, *"The sleep of a working man is pleasant, whether he has little or much. But the stomach of the rich man does not allow him to sleep." (Ecclesiastes 5:12, NAS)*

All the wealth and riches of this world cannot bring true contentment and does not satisfy. The pleasures of the riches of this world are short-lived. The rich people of the world often spend the majority of their time worrying about their acquired riches. They worry about their stocks, bonds and other investments and about maintaining their lavish lifestyle or striving to acquire more. They have no time to really enjoy what they have acquired.

GET YOUR EYES OFF YOUR LACK AND ONTO GOD'S UNLIMITED RESOURCES!

On the other hand, God gives His people the power…the ability…to enjoy the fruit of their labor, to enjoy the abundance of His blessings upon their lives.

One of Satan's major strategies in attacking your finances is to cause you to keep your eyes on your financial needs and problems, until you do not look to God for His supernatural provision in your life. Instead of looking to God for His supernatural provision, Satan wants you to look to the natural and to your own limited resources.

Satan will attack your finances and cause you to doubt God's care and provision instead of trusting Him to be faithful to His Word.

Satan wants you to keep your eyes on the large sum of money you owe…on your overdue bills…on your paycheck…on your bank account…on man-made solutions. He wants you to keep your eyes on your LACK…LACK of money, LACK of clothing, LACK of a good car, LACK of furniture, LACK of the things your children need.

The time has come for God's people to get their eyes off the natural…off themselves…off their paychecks…and get them on a supernatural God Who stands ready to supernaturally provide for their needs!

God planned that there be NO LACK in His House. He made every provision through His covenant that all your needs be met, that you PROSPER in every area of your life and in all that you do.

In His relationship with the children of Israel, God planned that they would experience His supernatural provision. During the forty years in the wilderness, He supernaturally led them by a pillar of cloud by day and a pillar of fire by night.

He rained manna from heaven, caused water to gush out of a rock and met all their needs. Their clothes did not wear out nor did their feet swell during the entire forty years! When they entered the promised land, they were not poor or sickly. They went with the riches of Egypt and there was not one feeble person among them! *"He brought them forth also with silver and gold: and there was not one feeble person among their tribes."* *(Psalm 105:37)*

The disobedient generation died in the wilderness but God brought a new generation in to possess His promises.

God caused the children of Israel to wander in the wilderness and fed them with daily manna to teach them not to depend upon themselves, but look to Him for His supernatural provision.

God does not want you to live in the natural realm where you look at your lack and depend upon man's limited resources to meet your needs. He wants you to live by the Word…according to His promises.

Get your eyes off your lack!

Get them off your needs!

God wants to give you a financial breakthrough where you are living in a cycle of His supernatural provision; where you trust Him to supernaturally meet your needs and there will be NO LACK!

Determine now in your heart, to remember God as your Source of supply, and continually seek after Him…to know Him in His unlimited power…to know His will…to acknowledge His blessings, and honor Him through your giving.

Remember God's faithfulness.

Remember the blessings He has poured into your life.

Remember the promises He has given you.

As long as you remember God and keep seeking after Him with your whole heart, He will fulfill His Word and will bless and prosper you.

BLESS
HEBREW – "barak". This word occurs 330 times in the Bible. It means, "to bestow good upon". God's ultimate purpose from the very beginning of His dealings with man, in the Garden of Eden, was to bless and prosper His people. God is the Source of all blessing. He raised up a chosen people, entered into a covenant with them and pronounced His blessings upon them. God's blessings rest upon His people today, who are the seed of Abraham through Christ and who are faithful to Him. (Galatians 3:14, 16, 29)
GREEK – "eulogeo" This word means, "to cause to prosper, to make happy, to bestow blessings on." God sent Jesus to bless us through salvation. (Acts 3:26) We have been blessed with all spiritual blessings in Christ and have inherited the blessing of Abraham. (Ephesians 1:3)

God will smite your enemies! *"The Lord shall cause thine enemies that rise up against thee to be smitten before thy face: they shall come out against thee one way, and flee before thee seven ways."*

Deuteronomy 28:7

SECTION 1 (A)

REMEMBER GOD AS YOUR SOURCE

WORKSHEET

1. In the space below, list the creditors and amounts of the most outstanding debts you owe:

   _____

   _____

   _____

   _____

   _____

   Ask yourself, "Am I depending solely upon my income and natural wisdom, abilities and resources to pay off these debts. Or, am I recognizing God as my Source and depending upon Him to release the finances I need?"

   ❏ I depend solely upon my natural resources and abilities.

   ❏ I look to God as my Source and depend upon Him to supernaturally provide and enable me to pay these debts.

2. When unexpected expenses or emergency expenditures arise do I look to my natural resources or do I pray and trust God and stand on His Word believing He will meet my needs?

   ❏ I depend upon my limited natural resources.

   ❏ I keep my eyes on God, pray and trust Him to supply the extra funds.

3. In your current financial circumstances, how much time do you and family members devote to talking about your **lack** of sufficient income, clothing, furniture and other basic needs, instead of focusing on God who stands ready to meet your needs? Check the answer that most applies to your circumstances.

   ❏ Constantly   ❏ Seldom

   ❏ Frequently   ❏ Never

4. When the children of Israel entered the promised land and began to enjoy the blessings God had provided for them, houses, lands, vineyards and bountiful harvests, they **forgot** God's miraculous provision. Instead of remembering God as their Source of Supply, they were filled with pride and began to say in their hearts, *"My power and the might of mine hand hath gotten me this wealth." (Deuteronomy 8:17)*

   God wants you to remember that it is He who provides for you and your family. It is easy to become so caught up in making a living and providing for your family that you forget that it is God Who is your Source and Who blessed you with all that you have.

   Remember specific occasions when God intervened in your time of need and sent unknown resources to meet that need. Remember how God has enabled you to meet unexpected expenses when you did not know where you were going to get the money. Remember the instances when God enabled you to find the job you needed, helped you buy your home, etc.

   Write these instances of God's provision down in the space below:

   _____

   _____

   _____

   _____

   _____

   _____

   _____

   _____

5. Set aside a specific time to gather your family around and praise God for His provision and faithfulness in meeting your needs. Ask Him to forgive you for all the times you have forgotten how He has provided for you and any time you have murmured about your lack.

6. Type or write the following Scripture on a card and place a copy of it in your wallet and checkbook as a continual reminder to look to God as your Source.

   "But thou shalt remember the Lord thy God: for it is he that giveth thee power to get wealth, that he may establish his covenant which he sware unto thy fathers as it is the day." (Deuteronomy 9:8)

The Lord will cause your enemies to be smitten before your face

7. SMITE YOUR FINANCIAL ENEMY!
Make a list of all your financial needs and all your possessions.

_____
_____
_____
_____
_____
_____
_____
_____
_____

Then: Recognize God has smitten your enemy!

And say out loud:

"The Lord shall cause thine enemies that rise up against thee to be smitten before thy face: they shall come out against thee one way, and flee before thee seven ways."

Deuteronomy 28:7

❑ I am believing God – lack, debt, defeat are my enemies.
Here is my "Smite My Enemies" gift of faith $_____.

Clip and mail this sheet to Morris Cerullo World Evangelism for Morris and Theresa Cerullo to join in a prayer of agreement for God to smite your financial enemies.

Morris Cerullo World Evangelism

U.S	**Canada**	**U.K.**
P.O. Box 85277	P.O. Box 3600	P.O. Box 277
San Diego, CA 92186	Concord, Ontario L4K 1B6	Hemel Hempstead, Herts

CLIP AND MAIL

KNOW GOD'S PLAN TO PROSPER YOU

I know the plans I have for you. Declares the Lord, plans to prosper you and not to harm you, plans to give you hope and a future.

Jeremiah 29:11, NIV

SECTION 1 (B)

KNOW GOD'S PLAN TO PROSPER YOU

As you develop your master financial plan, you must have a solid scriptural foundation concerning God's will for your finances. If you are not convinced it is God's will to supply your needs and prosper you, when Satan attacks your finances, you will begin to waver.

You will begin to worry.

Doubt and fear will fill your heart and mind.

Then, you will be unable to release your faith to have your needs met.

Are you convinced that it is God's will to prosper you? A great majority of Christians today are still not convinced that God is concerned about their finances and that it is His will to bless and prosper them. They have faith to believe God for the greatest miracle of all…the salvation of their souls. They have faith for the healing of their physical bodies. But they have not received a breakthrough in believing that God will also meet their financial needs.

The Hebrew word, "tsaleach" occurs 65 times in the text of the Old Testament. It means, "to succeed, prosper". The Greek word, "euodoo" means "to help on one's way." It also means, "to prosper, be prospered."

True prosperity is not the accumulation of wealth or the material things of this world, such as luxury cars, expensive homes, jewelry and designer clothes. That is the world's concept of prosperity.

The true prosperity God has planned for you is much more! It is the abundance of His blessings, both spiritual and temporal, which include health, protection, spiritual riches, provision for your needs as well as material blessings.

God's prosperity is total well-being, spirit, soul and body!

"Beloved, I pray that you may prosper in every way and [that your body] may keep well, even as [I know] your soul keeps well and prospers."

3 John 2, AMP

In this verse, John was writing to a believer named Gaius, who was faithfully supporting and ministering to the needs of believers and evangelists who were preaching the Gospel. John spoke this blessing over him because of his faithfulness in giving. When John expressed this desire that Gaius prosper and be in health, even as his souls prospered, he expressed God's will for all His people today.

God's Word is filled, cover to cover, with promises of the blessings and supernatural provision that He has planned for us to enjoy.

A strong example of God's desire to bless His people today is His promises to the children of Israel. He entered into a covenant with them and promised to bless and prosper them above the nations of the earth.

Look at God's promises of prosperity below:

"And it shall come to pass, if thou shalt hearken diligently unto the voice of the Lord thy God, to observe and to do all his commandments which I command thee this day, that the Lord thy God will set thee on high above all nations of the earth: And all these blessings shall come on thee, and overtake thee, if thou shalt hearken unto the voice of the Lord thy God. Blessed shalt thou be in the city, and blessed shalt thou be in the field. Blessed shall be the fruit of thy body, and the fruit of thy ground, and the fruit of thy cattle, the increase of thy kine, and the flocks of thy sheep. Blessed shall be thy basket and thy store. Blessed shalt thou be when thou comest in, and blessed shalt thou be when thou goest out. The Lord shall cause thine enemies that rise up against thee to be smitten before thy face: they shall come

out against thee one way, and flee before thee seven ways. The Lord shall command the blessing upon thee in thy storehouses, and in all that thou settest thine hand unto; and he shall bless thee in the land which the Lord thy God giveth thee. The Lord shall establish thee an holy people unto himself, as he hath sworn unto thee, if thou shalt keep the commandments of the Lord thy God, and walk in his ways. And all people of the earth shall see that thou art called by the name of the Lord: and they shall be afraid of thee. And the Lord shall make thee plenteous in goods, in the fruit of thy body, and in the fruit of thy cattle, and in the fruit of thy ground, in the land which the Lord sware unto thy fathers to give thee. The Lord shall open unto thee his good treasure, the heaven to give the rain unto thy land in his season, and to bless all the work of thine hand: and thou shalt lend unto many nations, and thou shalt not borrow. And the Lord shall make thee the head, and not the tail; and thou shalt be above only, and thou shalt not be beneath; if that thou hearken unto the commandments of the Lord thy God, which I command thee this day, to observe and to do them."

Deuteronomy 28:1-13

In these verses, we see God's purpose to bless and prosper His people clearly revealed. In verse one, we see His desire to set His people above other people upon the earth. God has planned to pour out His blessings upon you to such a degree that the world will see His provision in your life and know that He has prospered you.

In verses three through seven, God's blessings are listed, which cover every area of your life. He intends for His blessings to be upon you wherever you go; for your children and grandchildren to be blessed; for you to be blessed on your job; and that everything you set your hand to will be blessed.

Now is the time for those blessings to be released into your life! God is releasing an end-time financial anointing. God does not intend you to struggle to obtain these blessings. He promised that all these blessings will "overtake" you. (verse 2) In other words, you can expect them to come running after you! You are not going to search after them or struggle to receive them. God's promised blessings will search you out and overtake you!

God promised that He will COMMAND His blessing upon all that belongs to you, and in everything that you undertake. When God commands His blessings upon you and all that you possess, there is absolute certainty that it will happen. When the God Who commanded the stars, moon and sun into existence issues a decree from heaven to bless, absolutely nothing will be able to stop it!

In verse eleven, we again see God's promise of prosperity: "...the Lord shall make thee plenteous in goods." In the New American Standard version, this verse translates, "...the Lord will make you abound in prosperity."

God did not plan for you to barely survive, or to struggle and worry about how you will pay your bills, or how you will make it from one paycheck to another. He did not plan for you and your family to suffer from a lack of food or clothing, or the other necessities of life.

You may be retired, a widow or widower, on a fixed or very limited income and struggle from month to month just to pay your rent or house payment, pay utilities and put food on the table. There is very little or no money left to make necessary repairs, pay doctor bills or buy other basic necessities.

If you are a single parent working long, hard hours to support a family on a meager salary, no doubt you have spent many hours worrying...trying to find a way to survive...living from day to day, wondering how you are going to make it through another day.

God did not plan for you to be bound by mounting financial pressures, but that you will have a CONTINUAL SUPPLY of His blessings flowing into your life. He has planned for you to live every day **expecting...looking...believing** Him to supernaturally provide for your needs.

You may be a businessman facing the financial pressures of keeping your business going...loss of income...deficits...large overdue payments. God's will is that His blessings be poured out upon you, and that you and your business will PROSPER and INCREASE, so that your needs will be met and you will be able to sow more into the Kingdom of God.

The key to the release of God's blessing into your life is dependent upon two things: **your act of faith, and your obedience to God.** Look at verse one. Moses told the children of Israel, *"And it shall come to pass, if thou shalt hearken diligently unto the voice of the Lord thy God, to observe and to do all his commandments."* In verse two, he told the people that all these blessings would run after and overtake them *"...if thou shalt hearken unto the voice of the Lord thy God."*

If Satan can cause you to disobey and fail to walk according to what God directs you to do in honoring Him with your substance, you will be unable to receive the fulfillment of His promised blessings. This is where the real battle takes place.

As you plan your finances, you must have this truth, that God desires to prosper you, deep in your spirit as a strong foundation. If you rely on your natural mind instead of acting in faith upon God's promises, you will not be able to live in God's supernatural provision.

MAKE IT YOUR GOAL TO HONOR GOD WITH YOUR WEALTH

In your financial plan you need to incorporate as one of your strategies, knowing and acting on God's promises regarding His financial provision. You must get your eyes off your circumstances and begin meditating upon God promises. You must begin to confess the promises into your circumstances.

However, **claiming** God's promises and **appropriating** them in your life are not the same. Claiming God's promised blessings is not enough to give you the financial breakthrough you need. You must take the third step TO HONOR GOD WITH YOUR "SUBSTANCE"...whatever He has given you.

Many Christians today are frustrated and don't understand why they are not reaping God's promises of blessing and prosperity. They are claiming His promises but they are not following the principles God established concerning giving. As a result of not honoring God with their substance, they are not reaping God's promises.

God prospers and blesses us **as we honor Him with our substance**...with the wealth he has placed in our hands. Regardless of your income or what you possess...whether it is a large or small amount, God expects you to honor Him with it.

Look at the following verse:

"Honor the Lord with thy substance, and with the firstfruits of all thine increase: So shall thy barns be filled with plenty, and thy presses shall burst out with new wine."
                                                    Proverbs 3:9-10

The word "plenty" in verse ten means "fullness; abundance." The Hebrew root word is "to become satisfied." The expression "so shall thy barns be filled with plenty" depicts the greatest possible abundance.

When we honor the Lord with our substance, God promised to not only supply our needs, but to bless us with PLENTY...the greatest possible ABUNDANCE. Are you ready for God to bless you with the greatest possible abundance?

We do not have the right and cannot expect to reap God's blessings if we are not faithful in our giving to God. This may be hard for some people to accept, but it is true. We cannot expect God to deliver us out of financial bondage, and prosper and bless us when we fail to be good stewards of what God has given us. When we fail to live according to God's will concerning our finances, we open the door for Satan to attack us.

All of God's blessings that He promised to the children of Israel were based upon their obedience. They were given a choice: if they were obedient to God they lived under an "open heaven" and were blessed.

Moses told them: *"But if you will not obey the voice of the Lord your God; being watchful to do all His commandments and His statutes which I command you this day, then all these curses shall come upon you and over take you." (Deuteronomy 28:15, TAB)*

Giving of their "substance"...of all they possessed, was a means of honoring God as the Source of their blessing. As long as they were faithful and obedient in giving their tithes and offerings, they prospered. But when they forgot God and withheld from giving to Him, they reaped the curses.

The same principles that God established concerning giving apply to us today. Beloved, we have the same choice:

- To Honor God with our substance by giving our tithes and offerings; receive His supernatural provision and prosper and be blessed, or

- To withhold our finances from God and fail to receive His promised blessings.

The choice is yours.

If you want to live in a cycle of God's supernatural provision, you must make a commitment to honor God with the finances He has given you.

PROSPER

HEBREW – "tsaleach" This word occurs 65 times in the text of the Hebrew Old Testament. It means, "to succeed, prosper." God set His people above all other people on the face of the earth and poured out His blessings upon them. As long as they were obedient and faithful to Him they prospered in all the works of their hands. They succeeded in all their endeavors. Their crops were plenteous. Their livestock was healthy and multiplied. Their children were blessed. They were healthy and enjoyed a long, fruitful life filled with His abundance.

GREEK – "euodoo" The literal translation of this word is "to help on one's way". It also means "to prosper, be prospered". True prosperity is neither the accumulation of wealth nor the material things of this world, such as expensive cars, luxury homes, jewels and expensive clothes. That is the world's concept of prosperity.

The true prosperity that God plans for His people to enjoy today is much more! It is the abundance of all His blessings, both spiritual and temporal, which includes health, protection, spiritual riches, and provision for your needs as well as material blessings. His prosperity is total well being, spirit, soul and body!

SECTION 1(B)

KNOW GOD'S PLAN TO PROSPER YOU

WORKSHEET

1. What is the definition of prosperity?
    Discuss this question with your spouse and family. Write your definition down below:

    Prosperity is: _____
    _____
    _____
    _____
    _____
    _____

    Now, compare this with the world's concept of prosperity.

    The world's concept of prosperity is: _____
    _____
    _____
    _____
    _____

    What does God's Word reveal about true prosperity?_____
    _____
    _____
    _____
    _____

2. Know God's promises to prosper you. Study the following Scriptures and memorize them. Claim them and appropriate them in your life and in your finances.

TWELVE PROMISES OF GOD TO PROSPER ME

(1) The Lord will cause me to abound in prosperity:
  "And the Lord will make you abound in prosperity, in the offspring of your body and in the offspring of your beast and in the produce of your ground, in the land which the Lord swore to your fathers to give you."
                    Deuteronomy 28:11, NAS

(2) The Lord will open His storehouse and bless all the work of my hands:

"The Lord will open for you His good storehouse, the heavens, to give rain to your land in its season and to bless all the work of your hand; and you shall lend to many nations, but you shall not borrow."

Deuteronomy 28:12, NAS

(3) The Lord will command His blessings upon finances and all that I do:

"The Lord shall command the blessing upon you in your storehouse, and in all that you undertake; and He will bless you in the land which the Lord your God gives you."

Deuteronomy 28:8, AMP

(4) The Lord will bless me with an abundance:

"Honour the Lord with your capital and sufficiency [from your righteous labors], and with the first fruits of all your income. So shall your storage places be filled with plenty, and your vats be overflowing with new wine."

Proverbs 3:9-10, AMP

(5) God's blessing will enable me to enjoy true riches:

"The blessing of the Lord, it makes [truly] rich, and He adds no sorrow with it, neither does toiling increase it."

Proverbs 10:22

(6) God plans for me to be prosperous and successful:

"Do not let this Book of the Law depart from your mouth; meditate on it day and night, so that you may be careful to do everything written in it. Then you will be prosperous and successful."

Joshua 1:8, NIV

(7) God will throw open the floodgates of heaven and pour out such a blessing I will not be able to contain it:

"Bring the whole tithe into the storehouse, that there may be food in my house. Test me in this, "says the Lord Almighty," and see if I will not throw open the floodgates of heaven and pour out so much blessing that you will not have room enough for it."

Malachi 3:10, NIV

(8) God plans for me to prosper in everything I do:
"BLESSED IS the man who does not walk in the counsel of the wicked or stand in the way of sinners or sit in the seat of mockers. But his delight is in the Lord, and on his law he meditates day and night. He is like a tree planted by streams of water, which yields its fruit in season and whose leaf does not wither. Whatever he does prospers."
Psalm 1:1-3, NIV

(9) God plans for me to prosper in every way:
"Beloved, I pray that you will prosper in every way and (that your body) may keep well, even as [I know] your soul keeps well and prospers."
3 John 2, AMP

(10) God plans for me to have His continual provision and total supply:
"And God is able to make all grace (every favor and earthly blessing) come to you in abundance, so that you may always and under all circumstances and whatever the need, be self-sufficient – possessing enough to require no aid or support and furnished in abundance for every good work and charitable donation.
2 Corinthians 9:8, AMP

(11) God plans for me to receive blessings that will run over me:
"Give, and it shall be given unto you; good measure, pressed down, and shaken together, and running over, shall men give unto your bosom. For with the same measure that ye mete withal it shall be measured to you again."
Luke 6:38

(12) God plans for me to have a liberal supply:
"And my God will liberally supply (fill to the full) your every need according to His riches in glory in Christ Jesus."
Philippians 4:19

3. Review your giving to the Lord this year. Did you honor Him with your substance – the wealth He has given you?
Ask yourself the following questions:

a. Do I give indiscriminately, without first seeking God and what He wants me to give?

❏ Yes ❏ No

b. Do I honor God by giving Him the very best of all that I have?
❏ Yes ❏ No

c. Do I give haphazardly whenever I have the finances, instead of givingconsistently and putting God first?

❏ Give haphazardly   ❏ Put God first and give consistently

d. Do I give freely to God expecting and believing Him to release His provision into my life?

❏ Yes   ❏ No

ESTABLISH YOUR PRIORITIES

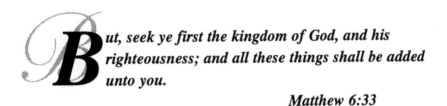

*B**ut, seek ye first the kingdom of God, and his righteousness; and all these things shall be added unto you.***

Matthew 6:33

Section 1(C)

ESTABLISH YOUR PRIORITIES

God wants you to walk in financial freedom and victory where there is no room for worry or doubt, because you KNOW that God will supernaturally provide ALL your needs.

This is God's time to release an end-time financial anointing upon you that will not only meet your current financial needs but will enable you to live in a cycle of God's supernatural provision where you reap God's abundance and all your needs are continually met.

Are you ready to put all your worries concerning your finances to rest?

Are you ready to break the financial bondage off your finances once and for all?

God does not want you to worry or be anxious about the things you need in your life. He has already provided for them in His Covenant with you.

God wants you to have fresh revelation of His DIVINE SUFFICIENCY that he has made possible for you to enjoy.

A major problem hindering many Christians from walking in the financial victory that Christ provides is that THEY HAVE THEIR PRIORITIES BACKWARD. Instead of seeking the Kingdom of God and putting it first and foremost in their lives, they seek to meet their own needs first. The vast majority of their time is spent acquiring the basic necessities of life. They spend their lives striving and worrying about providing for their families and "making ends meet."

It is time to get the mask off! Do you put the Kingdom of God first and foremost in your life? Do you spend more time seeking after God and His righteousness than you spend with the cares of this life?

Putting God first is one of the most important Laws of the Spiritual Harvest. When you put God first in every area of your life, when you put the

49

work of God above your own personal needs and desires and give God your very best first, you are planting "good seed" that will produce a bountiful harvest in which God will provide the things you need.

As long as you keep God first in your giving, you will never have to worry because Jesus said all the necessities of life will be added unto you. You will not worry because you will have His continual provision. Whenever you face a need, you will know that God will meet that need!

STOP WORRYING AND RELEASE YOUR FAITH!

In His Sermon on the Mount, Jesus introduced a life-changing principle, which assures us that God will provide all our daily needs. Immediately after giving us the admonition not to store up treasures for ourselves on earth and establishing the fact it is impossible to serve God and money, Jesus directs us not to worry concerning the basic, physical needs we have such as shelter, food, clothing and other necessities of life.

Jesus said:

"Therefore I tell you, do not worry about your life, what you will eat or drink; or about your body, what you will wear. Is not life more important than food, and the body more important than clothes? Look at the birds of the air; they do not sow or reap or store away in barns, and yet your heavenly Father feeds them. Are you not much more valuable than they? Who of you by worrying can add a single hour to his life? And why do you worry about clothes? See how the lilies of the field grow. They do not labor or spin. Yet I tell you that not even Solomon is all his splendor was dressed like one of these. If that is how God clothes the grass of the field, which is here today and tomorrow is thrown into the fire, will he not much more clothe you, O you of little faith? So do not worry saying, 'What shall we eat?' or 'What shall we drink?' or 'What shall we wear?' For the pagans run after all these things, and your heavenly Father knows that you need them."

Matthew 6:25-32, NIV

First, Jesus directs us **not to worry** concerning the basic, physical needs we have, such as shelter, food, clothing and the other necessities of life (verse 31).

As long as you worry about your needs, you will be unable to receive the financial breakthrough you need. When you worry, instead of releasing your faith and looking to God as your Source, you stop the flow of God's blessings and provision in your life. Your worry is a sign that you have not relinquished your needs into God's hands, but that you are trying to work out your financial problems yourself.

In verse 32, Jesus tells you why it is unnecessary to worry, *"...for your heavenly Father knoweth that ye have need of all these things."* Jesus did not say, "My heavenly Father. He said **"your"** heavenly Father. **"Your"** heavenly Father, Who is a GIVING GOD, Who loves to pour out His blessings upon His children, Who watches over you and is mindful of your every need, and even before you ask, is ready to meet your needs.

Your heavenly Father is just waiting for you to ASK IN FAITH. As long as you are bound by worry, you cannot go before your Father and ask in faith for the things you need. As long you are worried, fearful and doubting, you will be unable to receive anything.

The apostle James said, *"But let him ask in faith, nothing wavering. For he that wavereth is like a wave of the sea driven with the wind tossed. For let not that man think that he shall receive any thing of the Lord." (James 1:6-7)*

"But seek first his kingdom and his righteousness, and all these things will be given to you."
                                                    Matthew 6:33, NIV

All the things you need: food, clothing, shelter and all your daily needs will be supplied when you put God and His Kingdom **first!**

GIVING AND RECEIVING

In His Sermon on the Mount, Jesus introduced a new law of giving and receiving, which is the foundation for our giving today. It is based upon giving to God your very best **first**, and then RECEIVING back what God has multiplied...that which is running over!

"Give, and it shall be given unto you; good measure, pressed down, and shaken together, and running over, shall men give into your bosom. For with the same measure that ye mete withal it shall be measured to you again."
                                                    Luke 6:38

Giving, under the Old Covenant, was based upon the children of Israel **first receiving** from God His abundance, **and then giving** the firstfruits and tithe of all they received...**Receiving, then Giving.**

Under the New Covenant, all that we are and all that we have belongs to God. Our bodies are to be living sacrifices. (Romans 12:1) Above all else, God wants us to give ourselves to Him, unreservedly FIRST. Our time, our talents, our possessions and our finances belong to God. As we give our very best...of ourselves and our finances, God takes what we give, multiplies it, and gives it back to us. The pattern Christ established under the New Covenant is...**Giving, then Receiving.**

When you give to the work of God...to help build God an army in the nations of the world, to reach the nations of Israel with the Gospel of Jesus Christ as the Messiah, to support various ministries, to help the poor and needy or to minister to a brother or sister in the Lord who has a need, there is no reason you should worry or fear that you will suffer lack. There is no room for doubt. Jesus simply said, "Give, and it will be given to you". It is not a question of "maybe"; it is a matter of fact. Just as surely as a farmer knows when he plants a seed in the ground that it will grow, you can know that when you give you will receive.

Notice the type of return you can expect to receive when you give, **"...good measure, pressed down, and shaken together, and running over."** Can you take this kind of blessing? Running over means overflowing. God's blessing will overflow into your life...not just in your finances, but in your family, on your job, in every area of your life.

The devil wants you to think that if you give, you will go needy or you will have insufficient funds left to take care of your needs and commitments. The truth is that when you give, God promised to give back to you, not just what you have given (dollar for dollar), but a blessing multiplied until it is running over!

The proportion that you receive is according to the measure that you use when you give. Jesus said, *"...For with the measure you use, it will be measured to you." (Luke 6:38, NIV)* If you give liberally in proportion to how God has blessed and prospered you, you will receive a liberal return. On the other hand, if you give very little in proportion to how God has blessed you, you can expect a small return.

GIVE EXPECTING TO RECEIVE FROM GOD'S UNLIMITED RESOURCES

Making God and His Kingdom first in your priorities is one of the most important steps you must take if you want to reap God's blessing and live in a cycle of His supernatural provision.

To establish God and His Kingdom as your number one priority, even before your own needs, means that the very first thing you must do whenever you receive your check is to give God your tithe. Do not look at your income and your bills first to determine if you have money to give God your tithe. Put Him first!

As you develop your financial plan, the first thing you need to do is to determine how much you are going to give to God. Do not measure your gift to Him by what you have left after you have paid your bills and met other needs.

Determine in your heart that you will give your tithes and special offerings first, above everything else. Seek God's direction and establish goals for your giving. Make your giving part of your monthly budget.

Many times, Christians give expecting to receive a return according to man's ability to give. When you give to God, you can expect to receive from Him, not according to man's limited ability, but according to His unlimited resources.

Not only can you expect to receive a return from God, you can know that He will multiply what you have given. He will give you such a blessing, it will be running over. Not only will you have what you need, you will have an abundance so that you will be able to sow more into God's work around the world.

ESTABLISH YOUR PRIORITIES

WORKSHEET

1. Review your giving to God for this year. Ask yourself, "Have I put giving to God first above my own needs and the needs of my family?

   ❏ Yes ❏ No

   Were you faithful in giving God your tithe (10% of your income)?

   ❏ Yes ❏ No

   Have you given special offerings above your tithe?

   ❏ Yes ❏ No

   Did you spend more money on personal needs and desires, entertainment and other activities than your gifts to God and His work?

   ❏ Yes ❏ No

2. In the space below, write down specific goals in your giving to God.
   For example: If you are currently giving your tithe (10%), you may want to establish a goal of increasing your giving to 12%.

   _____

   _____

   _____

   _____

   _____

   _____

   _____

   _____

MY COMMITMENT TO GIVING

I establish giving to God and building His Kingdom as my first priority, above my own needs and the needs of my family.

I dedicate my finances to God.

I will be willing and obedient to God in my giving.

I will worship God through my giving as an expression of my love.

I will give liberally to God's work, expecting and believing God to meet all my needs.

_____   _____
Date   Signed

MY GOALS FOR GIVING FOR _____
                                                  (Year)

Annual Income (gross) $ _____

Monthly Income (gross) $ _____

Total giving for last year $ _____

Total average giving for last year $ _____

**My goal is to increase my total
amount of giving this year to** $ _____

Insert the above amount of your projected giving on page 101 in Section Four – Develop Your Life Financial Plan, Under "Mission Giving."

**Tear out this page and mail to Morris Cerullo Today at:
U.S.: P.O. Box 85277 • San Diego, CA 92186-5277
Canada: P.O. Box 3600 • Concord, Ontario L4k 1b6
U.K.:P.O. Box 277 • Hemel Hempstead, HERTS HP2 7dh**

SPECIAL PROJECT GIVING

God has spoken to my heart to give for the following projects. I am believing Him to release extra funds to enable me to give these amounts. Morris Cerullo World Evangelism Seven Point Master Plan to reach souls is as follows: 1) Worldwide Mass Crusade & Schools of Ministry, 2) Jewish World Outreach, 3) God's Victorious Army & Prison Ministry, 4) Television Programs and Specials, 5) Global Satellite Network, 6) Global Prayer Covering, 7) Worldwide Literature, Training Manuals & Bible Distribution. You could not sow into more fertile ground.

Name of Special Projects	Amount of Gift
_____	$ _____
_____	$ _____
_____	$ _____
_____	$ _____
_____	$ _____
_____	$ _____
_____	$ _____
_____	$ _____
_____	$ _____

TOTAL $ _____

MY RECORD OF GIVING

FOR _____

(Year)

ANNUAL INCOME_____
TITHE (10%) _____
OFFERINGS _____
SPECIAL PROJECTS _____
TOTAL GIVING _____

Tear out this page and mail to Morris Cerullo Today.

CLIP AND MAIL

CLIP AND MAIL

CLIP AND MAIL

MONTHLY GIVING TO GOD

JAN	FEB	MAR	APR	MAY	JUNE	JULY	AUG	SEPT	OCT	NOV	DEC

My commitment of giving to my church: _____

_____

_____

_____

_____

_____

_____

_____

_____

_____

_____

_____

_____

_____

My commitment of giving to ministries that are "good soil" where souls are being won to the Lord: **(See MCWE's Seven Point Master Plan to reach souls under "Special Project Giving" on previous page.)** _____

_____

_____

_____

_____

_____

_____

_____

_____

_____

By God's grace, I will put Him first in my giving and fulfill these commitments.

_____   _____

Signed   *Date*

FOCUS ON YOUR GOD-GIVEN VISION

rite the vision and make it plain on tablets, that he may run who reads it.

Habbakuk 2:2, NKJV

FOCUS ON YOUR GOD-GIVEN VISION

One of the most important steps in developing a financial plan is to first focus on your God-given vision and what you believe God has called you to do.

A major mistake people often make in financial planning is that their primary focus is upon managing their assets and their current financial status instead of on aligning their finances in fulfilling their God-given vision and purpose.

If they are in debt, major concern and focus of their financial plan is debt reduction. While debt reduction is vitally important in an individual's life, this should not be the first consideration or the major focus.

God does not want to limit what He can do in your life according to your current financial situation. You may be deeply in debt and wonder how you will ever be able to fulfill the vision God has given you. Your major focus may be on just making ends meet and providing for the basic necessities of your family.

If you keep your focus only on your current financial situation and upon your limited income or lack of finances, you will never be able to step out in faith and dare to believe God to release the finances to enable you to fulfill your vision.

GOD WANTS TO CHANGE YOUR FOCUS!

As you develop your financial plan, He wants you to take the limits off Him. God is saying to you, "Is there anything too hard for Me? See Me and My unlimited power working on your behalf. Set your heart upon the goals and vision I have given you. Look to Me and see Me as I am. I will not fail you. I will fulfill My plan and purpose in your life as you commit your ways into My hands and place your trust in Me."

God is a God of purpose, plan, design and objectivity. He has a specific purpose for your life. Regardless of who you are, your age or natural limitations, He has given you abilities, talents and His anointing to fulfill that purpose.

What are the vision, purpose, goals and dreams God has given you?

If you are unsure about God's purpose for your life, set aside a specific time to seek God's direction. Spend time in prayer and in the Word. Ask God to reveal His purpose for you, what does He wants you to accomplish in this life for Him?

Commit and dedicate your life to fulfilling that purpose. Be willing to lay aside your own self-centered goals, desires and plans. Jesus said, *"Whoever wants to save his life will lose it, but whoever loses his life for me will find it."* (Matthew 16:25) Only as you fully surrender your life with your goals and plans for Christ's sake will you find life and live it to its fullest.

DEVELOP A LIFE PLAN

When you know God's purpose for your life, set your focus on fulfilling it. Develop a life plan and develop your financial plan that will enable you to see how much money it will take to reach your goals and vision.

With a life plan you will be focused and single-minded. Jesus' entire life was focused on fulfilling God's will. He said, *"My food (nourishment) is to do the will (pleasure) of Him Who sent Me and to accomplish and completely finish His work."* (John 4:34, AMP)

Without a life plan you will wander from goal to goal. You won't be focused and your life will be spent seeking after many unfinished dreams.

God may have called you to be a doctor with a purpose of helping people in underdeveloped nations. But having a life plan or God-given desire is not enough. You may have a heart of compassion for the poor in India and God has given you a vision to establish an outreach to feed and clothe the poor. However, if you do not have a plan drawn up to get you where you want to go – the training, education, the costs involved and a plan to get the money for it, you will more than likely not be able to fulfill your vision.

DEVELOP A FINANCIAL PLAN TO HELP YOU FULFILL YOUR VISION

Jesus taught the importance of counting the cost in fulfilling a vision.

He said:

"Suppose one of you wants to build a tower. Will he not first sit down and estimate the cost to see if he has enough money to complete it? For if he lays the foundation and is not able to finish it, everyone who sees it will ridicule him, saying, 'This fellow began to build and was not able to finish."

Luke 14:28-30, NIV.

In this parable, Jesus was talking about counting the cost when we become one of His disciples. We must be willing to make a wholehearted commitment and count the cost so that later, when the trials and battles come, we won't give up and quit.

What He taught in these verses also applies to the financial areas of your life. Once you are focused on the vision God has given you, you need to not only make a wholehearted commitment to fulfilling the vision, you need a life plan and a financial plan.

Millions of people set out to fulfill a goal or vision without planning properly or counting the cost and end up in serious debt, with their dreams crushed. Many times, when people are unable to reach their life's goals, they give up on their dreams or vision and settle for second best.

Where are you in fulfilling the God-given vision and purpose for your life?

Are you like the person in Jesus' parable who started "building a tower", pursuing the fulfillment of your vision – and you have been unable to finish it? Have you given up hope on your vision because of your debts and lack of adequate finances?

DON'T GIVE UP ON YOUR VISION!

As a child of God, He has promised to bless the work of your hands. It is His will that you prosper and be successful in all that you do.

Don't keep you eyes on your current financial situation and become discouraged thinking you will never be able to launch out and fulfill your vision. And, do not allow your current financial situation to hinder or limit you in seeking to fulfill your vision.

We serve an unlimited God! Dream big! Dare to believe God for what may seem impossible to you!

God may have placed in your heart the vision to build a halfway house for abused women, an orphanage, a church, a prayer tower or some other major outreach. Yet, in the natural you are currently in debt, have no savings and no natural means to fulfill your vision. Do not allow your current financial state dictate whether or not you will fulfill your vision.

Focus on your vision by developing a life plan. Develop your financial plan to enable you to count the costs and develop a plan to fulfill the vision. Set up a financial system that revolves around your vision and goals. Keep track of your changing net worth and review each years planned spending accordingly.

As you give yourself wholeheartedly to God and make a solid commitment to fulfilling His purpose and vision for your life, release your faith and believe Him to release all the finances and provision to accomplish it.

"Roll your works upon the Lord – commit and trust them wholly to Him; [He will cause your thoughts to be agreeable to His will, and] so shall your plans be established and succeed."

Proverbs 16:3, AMP

FOCUS ON YOUR GOD-GIVEN VISION

WORKSHEET

1. Write out your life mission statement. What is the vision God has given you for your life?
Complete the following statement:
God is a God of _____ _____ _____ and _____.

By identifying and writing out your mission statement it will enable you to focus your thoughts and plan your time and actions accordingly to fulfill your purpose. *"Write the vision and make it plain on tablets, that he may run who reads it."*
(Habbakuk 2:2, NKJV)

As you prepare your mission statement, consider the talents and natural abilities as well as the spiritual gifts God has given you.
(See 1 Corinthians 12:1-12 and Romans 12:6-8)

In two sentences, write down what you believe is God's purpose for your life. Identify the goal you believe you should aim your time, energy and money toward. Be as specific as possible.

One example of a Mission Statement could be: To reach and teach inner-city children and provide a safe place for them to enjoy recreation and learn about God's love. To help evangelize unreached people groups through my prayers and giving.

Write down your Mission Statement here and on the Life Plan on page 68. If you are married, both husband and wife should fill out their own mission statement.

MY MISSION STATEMENT: (Husband)

_____
_____
_____
_____
_____

MY MISSION STATEMENT: (Wife)

_____
_____
_____
_____
_____
_____

2. Determine your long-range and short-range goals. What are the goals you need to reach in fulfilling your vision?

   Using the Mission Statement example above, some short-range goals might be: To establish a weekly outreach to children in a neighborhood park. To do research and an in-depth study on the major problems inner-city children face.

   A long-range goal might be: To rent or buy a building where you can have a recreational center for underprivileged children.

3. Write down your personal goals, dreams and desires. What are the desires of your heart? *"Delight yourself in the Lord and he will give you the desires of your heart." (Psalm 37:4)*

   As you dedicate and commit your life wholly to the Lord and make Him your first priority, He will enable you to fulfill your personal goals and give you the desires of your heart.

   A personal goal may be to take your entire family on a vacation of a life-time to Israel. It may be to complete your college education or take voice lessons and professionally record a CD.

4. After you prayerfully develop a mission statement describing your goals, career, ministry outreaches and personal dreams, you need to determine three of four intermediate steps. For example, using the same mission statement above about providing a safe place for inner-city children to enjoy recreation and learn about God and His love for them, intermediate steps could include:

   (1) Attend classes and receive training in counseling and working with abused children.

   (2) Rent a temporary facility, purchase recreational equipment and open an outreach to children in an inner-city neighborhood.

5. Estimate how much each goal will cost. Look at the Life Plan on page 68. Then under "Monthly Savings," write what you need to save toward that goal each month. Under "Date Achieved," write the month and year you expect to have the full amount saved.

In your current financial situation, you may be under a heavy burden of debt and do not have any extra funds to allocate toward savings. In Section Three, "Identify Your Current Financial Status" you will be able to take inventory of your current financial status, and in Section Five, "Develop A Debt Reduction Plan," you will learn how to pay off your debts so that you will be able to focus on fulfilling your financial goals and the vision God has given you.

MULTIPLY

GREEK – "Plethuno." This word signifies to increase, to cause to multiply. Within God's Cycle of Supernatural Provision, a supernatural multiplication occurs. After the Day of Pentecost when the Holy Spirit was outpoured, there was a supernatural multiplication which took place as God added to the Church daily. "And the word of God increased; and the number of the disciples multiplied in Jerusalem greatly..." (Acts 6:7) "And believers were the more added to the Lord, multitudes both of men and women." (Acts 5:14)

This multiplication was not the result of man's efforts but God's. God multiplied the number of disciples, "And the Lord added to the church daily such as should be saved." (Acts 2:47) This is the type of multiplication which will occur in this end time harvest. We will see the greatest harvest and multiplication of souls in the next few years than the Church has ever seen. It will not be the result of man's efforts but will be a supernatural multiplication by God's Spirit.

There is also a supernatural multiplication that occurs when you give to God. Not only does God provide the seed for you to sow, but He multiplies back to you what you give until there is a divine sufficiency in your life! The multiplication that occurs is not according to man's measurement, but according to God's UNLIMITED SUPPLY. God multiplies what you give until there is abundant provision. Not only are your needs met but you have more to sow back into the Kingdom of God.

MY LIFE PLAN

"A man's mind plans his way, but the Lord directs his steps and makes them sure."

Proverbs 16:9, AMP

MISSION STATEMENT:

_____
_____
_____
_____
_____
_____

INTERMEDIATE GOALS (STEP):	TOTAL COST	MONTHLY SAVINGS	DATE ACHIEVED
1. _____	_____	_____	_____
2. _____	_____	_____	_____
3. _____	_____	_____	_____
4. _____	_____	_____	_____

SHORT TERM GOALS:
MINISTRY:

1. _____	_____	_____	_____
2. _____	_____	_____	_____
3. _____	_____	_____	_____

PERSONAL:

1. _____	_____	_____	_____
2. _____	_____	_____	_____
3. _____	_____	_____	_____

LONG TERM GOALS:
MINISTRY:

1. _____	_____	_____	_____
2. _____	_____	_____	_____
3. _____	_____	_____	_____

INTERMEDIATE GOALS (STEP):	TOTAL COST	MONTHLY SAVINGS	DATE ACHIEVED
PERSONAL:			
1. Auto	_____	_____	_____
2. College	_____	_____	_____
3. Wedding	_____	_____	_____
4. Buying a home	_____	_____	_____
5. Other	_____	_____	_____
RETIREMENT GOALS:			
1. _____	_____	_____	_____
2. _____	_____	_____	_____

MY CURRENT FINANCIAL STATUS:

1. Monthly Income   _____

2. Monthly Expenses   _____

*Spendable Income   _____

(Subtract monthly expenses from monthly

income to determine spendable income)

*Amount of money available to apply to savings to fulfill goals and life vision.

Life Mission Covenant

"I beseech you therefore, brethren, by the mercies of God, that ye present your bodies a living sacrifice, holy, acceptable unto God, which is your reasonable service."
Romans 12:1

Date:_____

I present myself to God as a living sacrifice and give myself wholly to Him. I surrender my life completely to His plan and purpose for my life.

I make a total commitment of my time, talents, abilities and finances to fulfill the vision He has given me. I am standing on God's Word and believing Him to provide the finances necessary to fulfill this vision.

_____
Signature

IDENTIFY YOUR CURRENT FINANCIAL STATUS

*N*ow this is what the Lord Almighty says:
Give careful thought to your ways. You have
planted much; but have harvested little. You eat,
but never have enough. You drink, but never have your fill.
You put on clothes, but you are not warm. You earn wages,
only to put them in a purse with holes in them.

Haggai 1:5-6, NIV

SECTION 3

IDENTIFY YOUR CURRENT FINANCIAL STATUS

Once you have a solid foundation from the Word concerning God's plan to prosper you, you have developed a mission statement and are focused on God's purpose for your life, you need to determine your current financial status. This will enable you to further develop God-given strategies to reduce debt and increase your savings toward the fulfillment of your goals.

To identify your current financial status, you need to look at your current income, saving your regular bills and total debts.

To find your net worth, add up your assets, the value of what you own and subtract your liabilities, the amount of debt you owe. This will give you a good beginning point to start your planning toward financial freedom. (Use the forms on pages 82-83)

It is a good practice to calculate your net worth at least once a year. You will be able to compare your progress as your net worth grows over the years and you will know what it is going to take to plan to reach and fulfill your goals.

As you take inventory of your current financial status, it is very important that you also take an honest look at your attitude concerning money, your pattern of giving as well as look closely at how you handle your finances. All of these things must be taken into consideration to enable you to break the bondage of debt and live in God's cycle of supernatural provision.

If you are not consistent in your giving to God and withhold your tithes and offerings, you will not be able to reap God's blessings upon your finances. And, if you have not developed good spending habits and do not have a plan or budget to help you stay on target in paying your debts and saving money, your finances will not improve. How can we expect God to release His blessings upon our finances, if we are not faithful and obedient in our giving and fail to be good stewards of what He has given us?

Determining where you are currently and preparing a budget are only the beginning. You must be willing to count the cost. How much do you desire to be debt free and have the necessary finances to fulfill the purpose and vision God has given you?

Taking control of your finances will require discipline. It will require bringing your spending habits under control; living within your means and not spending more than you earn; putting an end to impulse buying; and most importantly, keeping your commitment to God in your giving as your number one priority.

LIVE UNDER AN "OPEN HEAVEN"

You have a choice. To live under an "open heaven" where you live in full communion and fellowship with God and enjoy His blessings upon your life; or to live under a "closed heaven" where your communion with God is blocked and you no longer reap His blessings.

Living under an open heaven, you enjoy close fellowship and communion with God. When you pray, there is a distinct awareness that your prayers are getting through and that God has heard and will answer your prayers.

You live in God's cycle of supernatural provision. As you faithfully sow seed of yourself, your time, abilities and finances…your reap His blessings.

The key to living under an open heaven is your obedience to God and His Word, and your faithfulness through your giving. As long as you walk in obedience to God and remain faithful in worshiping Him through your tithes and offerings, you will continue to live under an open heaven.

Releasing is the key that opens the windows of heaven. As you release your faith, love and worship to God; and give according to the pattern God has established in His Word, the heavens, which once seemed as brass, will be thrown open and you will once again live under an open heaven where His blessings are flowing into your life.

Living under a closed heaven, your fellowship and communion with God is hindered. It seems God is distant and the heavens are brass and your prayers cannot get through. Your efforts and energies are cut off from the flow of God's blessings upon your life.

The reason for living under a closed heaven is disobedience and withholding from God. As long as you walk in disobedience, you are sinning against God and your communion with Him is broken. Confession and repentance are the keys to restoration of full communion with Him.

WITHHOLDING FROM GOD CLOSES THE WINDOWS OF HEAVEN

This is the number one worst thing you can do, especially when facing a financial slow down. Withholding from God closes the windows of heaven. When you withhold from God and fail to sow seed of yourself…your time, abilities and finances…you shut yourself off from the flow of His promised blessings.

God promised the children of Israel that as long as they would love, serve and obey Him, with all their heart, soul, mind and strength, they would live under an open heaven where He would pour out His blessings upon them and prosper them. He promised to send rain upon their crops and they would enjoy His total provision.

After the children of Israel entered the promised land, they forgot God and His promises. They stopped giving their tithes and offerings, and began worshipping idol gods of wood and stone. As a result, they lived under a closed heaven. God shut up the heavens. Instead of reaping the abundance and prosperity God promised, they lived in famine and poverty.

Satan's objective is to cause you to forget God, to doubt His love and provision for you. When you face financial difficulties, the enemy wants you to forget God's promises and His faithfulness to you. He wants you to forget the promises and prophecies so you will be unable to get your needs met.

There are times God will allow you to go through deep waters, through tremendous financial difficulties to prove you and see what is really in your heart. God says, "I want to know what's in your heart. I want to know how deep our relationship is, if you're sincere. I want to know if you're honest."

Giving to God opens the "windows of heaven" of God's blessings.

Withholding closes the "windows of heaven" of God's blessings.

These same principles God established concerning giving apply today.

There are many Christians who are in financial bondage because they have withheld their finances and are not giving as God directed. Withholding from God is what leads Christians into financial bondage and keeps them there.

"There are those who (generously) scatter abroad, and yet increase more; there are those who withhold more than is fitting or what is justly due, but it tends only to want. The liberal person shall be enriched, and he who waters shall himself be watered."

Proverbs 11:24-25, AMP

The majority of Christians today are in financial bondage because they have not been faithful and obedient to God and the principles He set forth regarding giving and receiving. Ninety percent of the Christians filling our churches today do not even give their tithes to God.

Withholding does not make God's Word and His promises of blessing and prosperity void; but it blocks the flow of those promises from being manifested in your life and leads to poverty.

GOD WILL THROW OPEN THE WINDOWS OF HEAVEN!

The major method God uses today to pour out His blessings upon His people is the tithe. Is it any wonder that this is the one area where Satan has hindered the majority of Christians from receiving God's promised blessings?

Satan has a two-fold purpose to bind and destroy your finances.

1. He wants to stop you from getting your needs met.

2. He wants to hinder you from financing the work of God in the nations of the world.

If the enemy can cause you to withhold in giving your tithe and offerings, he will succeed in binding your finances.

The key to reaping God's blessings upon your finances is in developing your relationship with Him; where you are walking in absolute obedience to the divine pattern He has established in His Word concerning giving and receiving.

In God's plan of supernatural provision, He intended for the tithe to be the means, whereby, He not only blessed and prospered His people, but also, whereby, the needs of the House of God were supplied.

"Bring the whole tithe into the storehouse, that there may be food in my house. Test me in this, "says the Lord Almighty", and see if I will not throw open the floodgates of heaven and pour out so much blessing that you will not have room enough for it."

Malachi 3:10, NIV

Your tithe, the tenth of all your income, belongs to the Lord. It is holy. It is precious seed, which you sow to reap His promised blessings.

God's challenge to you today is to prove Him. He wants you to test Him to see if His promise of blessing is true.

His storehouse is full of everything you need and more. He has stored up blessings upon blessings for you, far greater than anything you can think or ask. The answer to your financial needs is there, and God is just waiting to prove Himself to you.

GOD WANTS YOU TO PROVE HIM!

Too many Christians are waiting for God to meet their financial needs first. They are waiting for Him to increase their income first before they give their tithe. There are many who wait until after all their bills are paid and if there is any money left they will give their tithes.

God says, "Give Me your tithe FIRST, then prove me, to see if I will pour out My blessings upon you".

The type of blessing God has promised is not an ordinary blessing. It is not just enough for you to get by. He has promised to pour out a blessing upon you "that there shall not be room enough to receive it."

If you are faithfully and consistently giving God your tithe, you have God's promise as your guarantee that you will reap an abundant harvest where there is more than enough!

As you look at your current financial status, review your faithfulness to God in giving your tithe and offerings.

Think about the financial pressures and problems you face right now. Have you honored God with your substance by faithfully giving your tithe and offerings, even in the midst of these problems? If you have, you can face Satan's attacks against your finances from a position of strength, knowing God has entered into a covenant with you, and that none of His promises will ever fail!

If you have been withholding from giving your tithes and offerings to God, you need to repent and ask God's forgiveness. Then, regardless of the financial circumstance you face, break the financial bondage you are in by giving to God a tithe of your income and the largest offering possible.

As you do this, release your faith to God, knowing that He will supernaturally provide all your needs, open the "windows of heaven," and pour out His blessings and abundance upon you.

PROVE

HEBREW – "bachan" This word means "to examine, prove, to test."

GREEK – "dokimazo" which means, "to test with the expectation of approving."

God bound Himself to you with His Word. He promised to pour out His blessings into your life in abundance as you give your tithes. He put His Word on the line and said, "Prove Me!" As you give your tithes, do it with an expectation that He will fulfill His promise to you. Look for His blessings to come upon you. Expect the windows of Heaven to be opened to you! You do not need to wonder or question whether God will meet your need, PROVE HIM!

Regardless of the circumstances you may face right now, **God is saying to you: "Put Me first! Trust Me and My promises to you. Test Me! Prove Me! I will be faithful in opening the windows of blessing of My abundance to you. I am bound to you by My Word. You will receive all that I have promised as you remain faithful and obedient to Me!"**

IDENTIFY YOUR CURRENT FINANCIAL STATUS

WORKSHEET

1. Review your records from last year and your faithfulness in giving God your tithe.

   a. Each payday, did you write out your check or set aside the money for giving God your tithes first, before considering your own needs and expenses?

      ❏ Consistently   ❏ Occasionally   ❏ Never

   b. When you face major financial problems, do you withhold giving your tithe because you are fearful that you will not have enough to meet your needs and the needs of your family?

      ❏ Never   ❏ Withhold when   ❏ Am withholding
         withhold   facing financial   my tithe until I
         tithe   problems   receive more
                                                     money

   c. When you give your tithe, do you do it from a heart of love in true worship; or, has it become a matter of routine or just a religious exercise?

   d. If you have not been faithful in giving God your tithe – a tenth of your income – or if you are just giving Him your tithe as a religious duty, repent. Ask God to forgive you and make a new commitment to faithfully give your tithe as part of your worship.

2. Evaluate Your Spending Habits

   a. What are your best and worst financial habits?

      _____
      _____
      _____

   b. Do you ever buy things on impulse? ❏ Yes ❏ No

   Why? _____
      _____
      _____

c. Do you have a written budget that you stick to?

❑ Yes ❑ No

d. Do you set aside money, regularly, in a savings account?

❑ Yes   ❑ No

If no, why not? _____

_____

_____

_____

e. Do you set aside money to achieve specific goals?

❑ Yes ❑ No

f. Do you have a filing system to keep track of your financial records?

❑ Yes   ❑ No

g. Do you ever buy things to impress others or to gain love and acceptance?

❑ Yes   ❑ No

h. Do you pay off the entire balance on your credit card when it is due?

❑ Yes   ❑ No

i. Do you often buy things and charge them to your credit cards when you really can't afford it?

❑ Yes   ❑ No

j. When you purchase something, do you first ask yourself, "Do I really need this?" And "Do I have the extra money it will cost?"

❑ Yes   ❑ No

k. The majority of my spending is done with:

❑ Credit Cards   ❑ Cash   ❑ Checks

l.   When I use my credit cards:
   ❏   I never charge more than what I can pay in full each month.
   ❏   My credit cards are charged to the limit
   ❏   I make only the minimum required payment each month
   ❏   I sometimes borrow on one credit card to make payments
        on others.

m. What do you believe is the major reason why you are in debt?

   _____
   _____
   _____
   _____
   _____

n. Do you believe your spending habits and manner of handling your finances honors
    God and is pleasing to Him?   ❏ Yes❏ No

o.   What are some specific actions you can take to improve your
     spending habits?

   _____
   _____
   _____
   _____
   _____

3. To gain a clear understanding of where your money is going and a better understanding
    of your spending habits, track your expenses for a month.

    Use the form on page 87. Photo copy this form for more space. Write down every
    expenditure, and every purchase that you and your family make during the month.
    Include your tithe and offerings, mission gifts, as well as any personal gifts you may
    purchase. Keep all your receipts in an envelope so that you will be able to add them up
    at the end of the month. Right now, you may not realize where you are spending your
    money, but it seems as there is always little or no money left at the end of the month for
    savings or investments. At the end of the month, when this form is filled in, it will
    show you how you are actually spending your money so that you will be able to take the
    necessary actions to gain control.

IDENTIFY YOUR CURRENT
FINANCIAL STATUS

RECORD OF NET WORTH

Note: Calculate your net worth at least once a year. A good time to do this would be as you are preparing your taxes. This will enable you to monitor your progress and compare it as your net worth grows over the years. Make a photocopy of this form and file it to use next year as a comparison.

ASSETS (at sales value)

Cash (checking, money-market accounts,

savings, CDs)	$_____
Invested Assets	$_____
Insurance and Annuities	$_____
Stocks & Stock Mutual Funds	$_____
Bonds & Bond Mutual Funds	$_____
Partnerships	$_____
Residence	$_____
Other Real Estate	$_____
Notes and Trust Deeds	$_____
IRAs & Other Retirement Accounts	$_____
Other Assets	$_____
Total Invested Assets	$_____

Personal Assets

Furnishings	$_____
Automobiles	$_____
Collections	$_____
Other	$_____
Total Personal Assets	$_____
TOTAL ASSETS	$_____

LIABILITIES

Secured Liabilities

Mortgage on Residence	$_____
Automobile Loans	$_____
Notes and Trust Deeds	$_____
Loans Against Life Insurance	$_____
Other	$_____
Total Secured Liabilities	$_____

Unsecured Liabilities

Charge Account Balances	$_____
Bills Due	$_____
Personal Loans	$_____
Other	$_____
Total Unsecured Liabilities	$_____
TOTAL LIABILITIES	$_____

	_____
TOTAL ASSETS	$_____
– TOTAL LIABILITIES	$_____
= TOTAL NET WORTH	$_____

IDENTIFY YOUR CURRENT
FINANCIAL STATUS

INCOME

	Monthly Average	Annual
Take-home pay: Yourself	$ _____	$ _____
Your spouse	$ _____	$ _____
Self Employment	$ _____	$ _____
Second Job	$ _____	$ _____
Net income from rental property	$ _____	$ _____
Interest from savings account	$ _____	$ _____
Dividends from stocks & bonds	$ _____	$ _____
Alimony, Child support	$ _____	$ _____
Other	$ _____	$ _____
TOTAL:	$ _____	$ _____

1. Calculate your monthly take-home pay. Divide your annual net income by 12 months.

2. Determine your net spendable income by subtracting your tithe (10% of gross income) and your taxes.

NET SPENDABLE INCOME

	Monthly	Annual
GROSS INCOME PER MONTH	$ _____	$ _____
Tithe (10% gross income)	$ _____	$ _____
Tax	$ _____	$ _____
Net Spendable Income	$ _____	$ _____

MY CURRENT LIST
OF DEBTS

	Creditor or Account	% Rate (APR)	Payoff Amount	Payments Left	Monthly Amount	Due Date
01.						
02.						
03.						
04.						
05.						
06.						
07.						
08.						
09.						
10.						
11.						
12.						
13.						
14.						
15.						
16.						
17.						
18.						
19.						
20.						
21.						
22.						

IDENTIFY YOUR CURRENT
FINANCIAL STATUS

CREDIT CARD PAYMENTS

	Credit Card Account Name	Monthly Payments	Interst Rate	Balance Due
Card 01.				
Card 02.				
Card 03.				
Card 04.				
Card 05.				
Card 06.				
Card 07.				
Card 08.				
Card 09.				
Card 10.				
Card 11.				
Card 12.				

Note: List your current credit card debts with the largest balances toward the top (card 1) and smallest balances toward the bottom. Also, try to list the accounts with the highest interest rates toward the bottom of the list.

This chart will be helpful to you in developing your debt reduction strategies later in Section Five "Develop A Debt Reduction Plan".

MONTHLY EXPENSE TRACKING

WORKSHEET

Month of: _____

TOTAL   **INCOME**

Take home pay – Yourself $_____
Your spouse $_____
Bonuses (net) $_____
Self-employment Income $_____
Net Income from rental property $_____
Interest $_____
Dividends $_____
Alimony, Child Support $_____
Other: _____ $_____

_____

TOTAL $_____

EXPENSES

Date	Item	Amount	Budgeted? Yes	No
____	_____	_____	____	____
____	_____	_____	____	____
____	_____	_____	____	____
____	_____	_____	____	____
____	_____	_____	____	____
____	_____	_____	____	____
____	_____	_____	____	____
____	_____	_____	____	____
____	_____	_____	____	____
____	_____	_____	____	____

MONTHLY EXPENSE TRACKING

EVALUATION

At the end of the month, review your total expenses and answer the following questions:

1. What was your number one expense item with the largest amount spent?

    _____

    Why? _____

    _____

2. Did you purchase anything you really didn't need?   ☐ Yes ☐ No

    If yes, list your purchases here: _____

    _____

    _____

3. Subtract your total monthly expenses from your income. Did you have money left? ☐ Yes ☐ No

    If yes, where have you allocated it?

    ☐ Payment of outstanding debts

    ☐ Savings

    ☐ Other _____

4. Did you stay within your budget? ☐ Yes ☐ No

5. What do you think is your worst spending habit?

    _____

    _____

    _____

    _____

6. Write down specific strategies that will enable you to cut down on unnecessary spending:

    _____

    _____

    _____

    _____

    _____

7. Discuss with your family and determine what is the major areas of spending where you can cut back each month: _____

_____
_____
_____
_____
_____
_____
_____
_____
_____
_____
_____
_____
_____
_____

DEVELOP YOUR MASTER LIFE / FINANCIAL PLAN

And (God) Who provides seed for the sower and bread for eating will also provide and multiply your (resources for) sowing, and increase the fruits of your righteousness (which manifests itself in active goodness, kindness and charity).

2 Corinthians 9:10, AMP

DEVELOP YOUR MASTER LIFE / FINANCIAL PLAN

As stewards of God's money, it is our responsibility to develop a Life/Financial plan based upon the principles He has revealed in His Word. Recognizing God as your Source of supply, and knowing it is He who gives you the power to obtain wealth, you need to develop a plan that will enable you to not only reap a personal harvest in your finances, but also to fulfill His vision and purpose for your life.

Jesus emphasized a very important truth concerning good stewardship with our finances. He said, *"Whoever can be trusted with very little can also be trusted with much, and whoever is dishonest with very little will also be dishonest with much. So if you have not been trustworthy in handling worldly wealth, who will trust you with true riches?" (Luke 16: 10-11, NIV)*

God expects us to be faithful and plan wisely to make the best use of the finances He has entrusted to us.

Begin your planning by setting aside time to seek God's direction. If you are married, your plan must involve both husband and wife. Allocate at least one full day to pray and plan your finances for the year.

The first thing you must do, as you establish your budget, is to set your giving goals.

Why?

Because the key to receiving and your needs being met is your giving. And, the amount you receive is determined by the seed you sow. You will reap in proportion to what you sow. This is not a man-made theory. It is one of God's laws of the harvest.

"Remember this: whoever sows sparingly will also reap sparingly, and whoever sows generously will reap generously. Each man should give what he has decided in his heart to give, not reluctantly or under compulsion, for God loves a cheerful giver. And God is able to make all grace abound to you, so that in all things at all times, having all that you need, you will abound in every good work."

2 Corinthians 9:6-8, NIV

SOW! If you sow a small handful of corn or wheat in a field, you can expect a small harvest. On the other hand, if you sow several large barrels of seed, you will reap an abundant harvest. Your harvest is dependent upon the amount sown at seedtime.

All truth is parallel.

In the spiritual world, the same is true. One of the laws of the spiritual harvest is that you will receive IN PROPORTION TO WHAT YOU GIVE. When you give to God liberally, according to His plan and purpose, you can KNOW and EXPECT to receive from Him an ABUNDANT harvest. There is no question…no doubt. It is a fact! You can count on it.

DIVINE SUFFICIENCY

The proportion that you receive is according to the measure that you use when you give. If you give liberally in proportion to how God has blessed and prospered you, you will receive a liberal return. On the other hand, if you give very little in proportion to how God has blessed you, you can expect a small return.

In verse eight, God promised His DIVINE SUFFICIENCY. Circle the word "all" in this verse. Paul assured the believers in the Corinthian Church, as they gave this offering to meet the need of their brethren in the church in Jerusalem, they would have "ALL SUFFICIENCY IN ALL THINGS!"

The word "sufficiency" is translated from the Greek word "autarkeia", and in this verse is used to express the contentment which arises from the FULL SUPPLY of ALL our needs by God! God will cause His grace…His unmerited favor and blessings…to come to you in abundance, so that you will always…at all times and in all circumstances…have ALL SUFFICIENCY…a FULL SUPPLY…IN ALL THINGS.

Look at this verse in the Amplified version, which gives a clearer understanding of the original Greek, *"And God is able to make all grace (every favor and earthly blessing) come to you in abundance, so that you may always and under all circumstances and whatever the need, be self-sufficient — possessing enough to require no aid or support and furnished in abundance for every good work and charitable donation." (2 Corinthians 9:8, AMP)*

In these verses, Paul not only refers to spiritual, but also temporal blessings. As you give to God, He promises to pour out His blessings into your life in such abundance that you will lack nothing. There will be a DIVINE SUFFICIENCY in your life, so that there will be a continual flow of God's blessings where not only will all your needs be met, but you will also have more to give to God and His work.

Regardless of the financial needs you may be facing right now, God's promise to you is that as you are faithful in giving, He will meet those needs. Do not allow Satan to intimidate you and fill your mind with worry and doubt. Keep planting your seeds...keep giving to God...believing and expecting Him to fulfill this promise to use. Walk in His DIVINE SUFFICIENCY!

YOU ARE NOT LIMITED BY THE WEALTH AND RICHES OF THIS WORLD!

You do not need to rely on your own limited resources!

God is your source, and you have access to the resources of heaven!

The apostle Paul faced his circumstances depending on God as his source. In prison in Rome, he wrote to the believers in Philippi, who had given an offering to meet his needs, *"But I have all, and abound..." (Philippians 4:18)* How could he possibly say this? He did not have an abundance of the world's goods. He was in prison. But through his experiences...of facing times of hunger, nakedness and want...he had learned to depend on God, day by day, for His supernatural provision.

Paul wasn't worried about his circumstances. He didn't focus his eyes on his needs. He wasn't moaning, groaning, or complaining. In verses 11 and 12, he told the believers in the Philippian church, *"...I have learned to be content whatever the circumstances. I know what it is to be in need, and I know what it is to have plenty..." (Philippians 4:11-12, NIV)*

In the circumstances you face, can you say this?

Paul learned a secret of being content in every situation, whether living in plenty or in want. He wasn't looking to man to meet his needs; He was looking to God as his source. Because he knew God was his source, he was able to look at his circumstances, and say, *"I can do all things through Christ which strengtheneth me." (Philippians 4:13)*

Paul knew he wasn't going to be defeated because he was able to draw on his source to give him strength to overcome. Paul said to the Philippians, *"But my God shall supply all your need according to his riches in glory by Christ Jesus." (Philippians 4:19)* Circle the word "all" in this verse. He did not say some, but ALL. Whatever need you face is included under the word "all".

There are Christians today claiming this verse who are not seeing a manifestation of it in their lives because they are not freely and willingly giving to God first. Think about how foolish it would be for a farmer to go out into his fields day after day expecting to reap a harvest if he had never planted a seed.

This promise was given to the Philippians who first gave a sacrificial offering to meet Paul's need while he was in prison. What they had given to Paul, they had given to God. Not only did God see their sacrifice, but their offering ascended up into heaven as *"...an odour of a sweet smell, a sacrifice acceptable, wellpleasing to God." (Philippians 4:18)*

God received their offering, and Paul assured them God would recompense them by supplying ALL their needs. In these verses, Paul did not refer only to the spiritual riches, but to ALL needs, including physical and financial needs. He referred to your TOTAL WELL-BEING...spirit, soul and body.

Now, notice HOW God will supply ALL your needs.

"And my God will liberally supply (fill to the full) your every need according to His riches in glory in Christ Jesus."
Philippians 4:19, AMP

DRAW FROM GOD'S IMMEASURABLE SUPPLY

Paul did not say God will supply your needs according to the wealth of this world. He did not say God would supply them according to man's limited ability...but ACCORDING TO HIS RICHES IN GLORY IN CHRIST JESUS! God promised to supply all your needs, not from man's supply, but from His

UNLIMITED, IMMEASURABLE supply of riches and wealth far beyond your understanding.

Through Christ, God gave us ALL things. Why do we live so far below what He has provided for us? What do you need right now? Do you need strength? He will give you strength.

Do you need healing in your body? He will give it to you.

In your financial circumstances, what do you need? There is no need too great for Him. Whatever you need, He will give it to you! (Romans 8:32)

If you are faithfully and willingly giving to God according to His plan...planting seeds...God's promises of blessing and prosperity belong to you, and there is no question...no doubt...you **will** reap His abundance.

God promised *"The Lord will open for you His good storehouse, the heavens, to give rain to your land in its season and to bless all the work of your hand..." (Deuteronomy 28:12, NAS)*

Regardless of the needs you face, God's "storehouse" is never empty! God's storehouse is INEXHAUSTIBLE. Regardless of all your financial needs...regardless of all the needs of all of God's people, there is more than enough to supply all those needs with a vast surplus.

God's supply is never diminished. His supernatural supply is **IMMEASURABLE.** There is **abundance** and **total provision** for every need in your life. He is the Source of ALL blessing. Regardless of how many times you may draw from His storehouse what you need, there is always **more.**

As you plan your monthly budget, do not limit your goals for giving according to what you have left after paying your expenses. Remember, you will receive in proportion to the measure of what you give.

Giving your tithe is only the first step. A tenth of your income already belongs to God. Determine your goals for giving beyond just your tithe. You cannot outgive God!

ESTABLISH YOUR PRIORITIES AND GOALS

As you begin your financial planning, establish realistic, short-term and long-term financial goals. These goals will enable you to measure your progress and determine if adjustments are needed. (Use the form on page 105)

One of your major basic goals may be to be debt-free in one year. If you cannot realistically reach that goal in one year, you may be able to in two or three years.

Ask yourself, "What do I want to achieve in life?" "How will I be able to accomplish God's plan?"

In your planning, you also should establish a long-range plan for the surplus God supplies. Look forward to and expect God to pour out His blessings upon your finances. As you begin to receive His abundance, you need to have a plan in place to determine where it will go.

How much will you use to sow back into God's work? How much should you give to your family? How much will you invest?

As you plan your budget, establish priorities. Your long-range goals should focus on financial priorities. Discuss these priorities with your family and help your children understand the difference between needs, wants, and desires.

Needs are the purchases necessary to provide basic requirements such as food, clothing, medical coverage, etc. *"If we have food and covering, with these we shall be content." (I Timothy 6:8)*

Wants involve choices about the quality of goods to be used: dress clothes versus work clothes, lobster versus chicken, a used car versus a new one.

Desires are choices that should be made only after all the financial obligations are met.

DETERMINE YOUR CASH FLOW

To prepare your budget, begin by analyzing where your money is coming from and where it is being spent. Complete the Cash Flow Worksheet on pages 102-103.

List all available income, per month. Calculate your monthly take-home pay by dividing your annual income by twelve months. List all your fixed, monthly expenses as well as your variable expenses.

Compare your income and expenses. If your total income exceeds total expenses, you will only need to establish a method to control your budget and keep it on track. If your expenses exceed your income, you need to do an analysis of each budget area to determine where you can cut back.

PREPARE A MONTHLY BUDGET

Use the form on page 101 as a guideline to prepare your budget. At the top of the budget, include your Mission Statement. Also, insert the amounts you included on your Life Plan (page 68), which you need to save toward in fulfilling your God-given vision and purpose. Select one or more of your intermediate steps and budget monthly to save toward fulfilling those goals. Then, when you have saved enough to fulfill those goals, go back to your Life Plan and select one or more of the remaining goals.

Continue to do this in your budgeting process until you have accomplished all your goals.

ESTABLISH CHECKPOINTS TO MONITOR YOUR PROGRESS

Once your monthly budget is completed, you must take the next important step of implementing it. Once you have determined what you should be spending on each category every month, you need to establish checkpoints to measure your progress.

On your Life Plan (pg. 68) you indicated a projected time when you would like to have the money for each goal. Review them to make sure they are as realistic as possible.

Review your progress by logging your expenses and savings quarterly (every three months), as well as add them up once a year. (Use the form on page 104) Checking on your progress will enable you to see if you are still on track.

It is also good to establish a further checkpoint after five years. On your Life Plan, review your goals and choose one or more that you can reach in five years or less. On the Quarterly and Annual Budget Review, write down those goals in the 5-year space and the year it is to be completed. When you review your budget each year, determine your progress toward that goal. When you achieve it, write the next intermediate goal in it's place.

Developing, implementing and tracking your budget requires discipline, commitment, and diligence. Whatever you do, don't place your budget in a file somewhere and forget about it. You may not think that you have the time or the ability to keep track and monitor your budget. Ask God to give you His wisdom and understanding and to direct you.

As you take these important steps in financial planning, God will release His blessings. He will increase and multiply what you give until not only your

THE MORRIS CERULLO FINANCIAL PLANNER

needs will be met, but you will have an increase to be able to fulfill His purposes in your life.

SUPERNATURAL PROVISION

HEBREW – "mopheth". One of the words used in the Old Testament to refer to miracles is "wonder". Translated from this Hebrew word, it means "wonder, sign, portent", and is used to describe a divine act or a special display of divine power which supersedes the laws of nature. Our God is a God of signs, wonders and miracles! When He manifested His miracle-working power in delivering Israel out of Egyptian bondage, opening the Red Sea, manifesting His power and glory on Mount Sinai, raining manna from heaven, causing water to gush out of a rock, supernaturally delivering the children of Israel from their enemies and multiplying their crops, He was revealing His character as the All powerful God of signs, wonders and miracles. God desired His people to look to Him for His supernatural provision in their lives!

GREEK – "dunamis". This word refers to the supernatural, miracle-working power of God. Through the miracles Jesus performed in healing the sick, multiplying the fish and loaves, turning the water into wine, casting out demons, raising the dead, He revealed God's supernatural provision in meeting the needs of the people. The Church was born through the dunamis miracle-working power of God! Through the dunamis power of the Holy Spirit, He has imparted to the Church, He continues to manifest His miracle working power in supernaturally meeting the needs of His people. God's purpose for our lives is that we live in a cycle of His supernatural provision where we are continually expecting and looking to Him to supernaturally provide our needs.

LIFE / FINANCIAL PLAN BUDGET

WORKSHEET

MISSION STATEMENT:

_____

_____

_____

_____

GROSS INCOME:	**Annually**	$ _____
GROSS MONTHLY INCOME:		$ _____
Tithe (10% of income)		$ _____
Taxes		$ _____

NET MONTHLY INCOME

EXPENSES:

Housing (rental/house payment/utilities/maintenance)	$ _____
Food	$ _____
Auto (car payment, gas, maintenance)	$ _____
Insurance	$ _____
Total Debts	$ _____
Life Plan Goals (see page 62 in section 2. Select one or more of your Intermediate goals and insert amount for monthly savings Towards your goal.)	$ _____
Missions Giving	$ _____
Clothing	$ _____
Savings	$ _____
Medical / Dental	$ _____
Investments	$ _____
School/Child Care	$ _____
Entertainment / Recreation	$ _____
Miscellaneous	$ _____
MONTHLY TOTAL EXPENSES	$ _____

(Note: Total cannot exceed Net Monthly Income)

SECTION 4

MY CURRENT CASH FLOW

WORKSHEET

MY CURRENT CASH FLOW

Income	Monthly Average	Annual
Take-home pay – Yourself	$_____	$_____
Your Spouse	$_____	$_____
Bonuses (net)	$_____	$_____
Self-Employment Income	$_____	$_____
Net income from rental property	$_____	$_____
Interest	$_____	$_____
Dividends	$_____	$_____
Alimony, child support	$_____	$_____
Other _____	$_____	$_____
TOTAL	$_____	$_____

Fixed Expenses		
Tithe and other giving	$_____	$_____
Savings	$_____	$_____
Rent/house payment	$_____	$_____
Home insurance	$_____	$_____
Property taxes	$_____	$_____
Income and social security taxes		
Not withheld by employer(s)	$_____	$_____
Alimony, child support	$_____	$_____
Car insurance	$_____	$_____
Car payment	$_____	$_____
Student loan payment	$_____	$_____
Total installment and		
Credit card payments	$_____	$_____
Basic phone service	$_____	$_____
Utilities	$_____	$_____
Other _____		
	$_____	$_____
TOTAL	$_____	$_____

Adjustable Expenses	Monthly Average	Annual
Groceries	$ _____	$ _____
Entertainment	$ _____	$ _____
Clothes	$ _____	$ _____
Travel	$ _____	$ _____
Vacations	$ _____	$ _____
Medical, Dental bills	$ _____	$ _____
Gasoline	$ _____	$ _____
Furniture	$ _____	$ _____
Long-distance telephone	$ _____	$ _____
Trash	$ _____	$ _____
Cable TV	$ _____	$ _____
Laundry/dry cleaning	$ _____	$ _____
Music and other lessons	$ _____	$ _____
Educational expenses	$ _____	$ _____
Day care and babysitting	$ _____	$ _____
Personal care	$ _____	$ _____
Pocket money	$ _____	$ _____
Life insurance premiums	$ _____	$ _____
Hospitalization insurance	$ _____	$ _____
Disability insurance	$ _____	$ _____
Homeowner's/renter's insurance	$ _____	$ _____
Household maintenance & repairs	$ _____	$ _____
Yard maintenance and repairs	$ _____	$ _____
Donations to church, charities above Tithe	$ _____	$ _____
Subscriptions	$ _____	$ _____
Personal gifts	$ _____	$ _____
Other_____	$ _____	$ _____
_____	$ _____	$ _____
Adjustable Expense Total	$ _____	$ _____
+Fixed Expense Total	$ _____	$ _____
Total Expenses	$ _____	$ _____
Total Income	$ _____	$ _____
-Total Expenses	$ _____	$ _____
Surplus or Deficit	$ _____	$ _____

(Income minus expenditures)

SECTION 4

LIFE/FINANCIAL PLAN QUARTERLY BUDGET REVIEW

MISSION STATEMENT: _____

_____

_____

_____

Category	Month:		Month:		Month:		Total Budget	Total Actual	Goal
	Budget	Actual	Budget	Actual	Budget	Actual			
Tithe	$	$	$	$	$	$	$	$	$
Taxes	$	$	$	$	$	$	$	$	$
Housing	$	$	$	$	$	$	$	$	$
Food	$	$	$	$	$	$	$	$	$
Auto Total Expenses	$	$	$	$	$	$	$	$	$
Insurance	$	$	$	$	$	$	$	$	$
Debts	$	$	$	$	$	$	$	$	$
Life Plan Goals	$	$	$	$	$	$	$	$	$
Missions Giving	$	$	$	$	$	$	$	$	$
Clothing Savings	$	$	$	$	$	$	$	$	$
Medical / Dental	$	$	$	$	$	$	$	$	$
Investments	$	$	$	$	$	$	$	$	$
School Childcare	$	$	$	$	$	$	$	$	$
Entertainment /	$	$	$	$	$	$	$	$	$
Recreation	$	$	$	$	$	$	$	$	$
Miscellaneous	$	$	$	$	$	$	$	$	$
5-Year Goal	$	$	$	$	$	$	$	$	$
Total Expenses	$	$	$	$	$	$	$	$	$

(Note: Make 3 extra copies of this form so that you will be able track your monthly budget for a full year.

MY FINANCIAL GOALS

	Short-Term (within next year)	Medium-Term (within 5 years)	Long-Term (next 5-10 years)
Pay off credit cards	$ _____	$ _____	$ _____
Build up emergency reserve	$ _____	$ _____	$ _____
Buy a car	$ _____	$ _____	$ _____
Buy adequate insurance	$ _____	$ _____	$ _____
Increase giving to God's Work	$ _____	$ _____	$ _____
Fund IRA or Keogh Account	$ _____	$ _____	$ _____
Create college fund	$ _____	$ _____	$ _____
Save down payment for home	$ _____	$ _____	$ _____
Home improvements	$ _____	$ _____	$ _____
Take a dream vacation	$ _____	$ _____	$ _____
Start a business	$ _____	$ _____	$ _____
Make a charitable bequest	$ _____	$ _____	$ _____
Pay off mortgage early	$ _____	$ _____	$ _____
Achieve adequate retirement income	$ _____	$ _____	$ _____
Other_____	$ _____	$ _____	$ _____
_____	$ _____	$ _____	$ _____

SECTION 5

DEVELOP A DEBT ELIMINATION PLAN

nd I will restore to you the years that the locust hath eaten, the cankerworm, and the caterpillar, and the palmerworm, my great army which I sent among you. And ye shall eat in plenty, and be satisfied, and praise the name of the Lord your God, that hath dealt wondrously with you: and my people shall never be ashamed.

Joel 2:25-26

SECTION 5

DEVELOP A DEBT ELIMINATION PLAN

Are you a candidate for a miracle of debt cancellation?

Are you ready for God to break the bondage of debt and release His end-time financial anointing into your life?

Each of the steps you have taken in Sections 1-4 have been designed to bring you to a position of financial breakthrough whereby you are living in God's cycle of supernatural provision.

You are on your way to financial freedom!

Regardless of how much debt you owe, God will enable you to break free of all debt. You may look at your current debt and think it is impossible to ever be debt free. But remember you must not be bound by the limitations of your natural mind. By faith, you must begin to see yourself totally debt free. You must begin to take hold of God's promises and act according to what He has revealed in His Word. Begin to speak God's promises over your finances.

The first step you must take toward breaking the bondage of debt and reaping God's provision is to bind the spirit of fear from your mind.

Fear will keep you from taking a step of faith. It will cause you to withhold from giving to God. Fear that you will not have enough money to meet your needs or that you will not survive, will keep you from being faithful to God's Word.

You may think, "I have every right to be fearful...I have no income...I face bankruptcy...the bank is ready to foreclose on my house...I just do not know what I am going to do!"

Regardless of the circumstances you face, you must recognize fear as one of Satan's weapons to keep you living in a cycle of financial failure and defeat and reject it. (Look at the cycle of financial defeat on page 123)

As a child of God, fear has no place in your life! *"For God has not given us a spirit of fear but of power, love and a sound mind." (2 Timothy 1:7)* You serve the same God Who supernaturally provided for His people and prospered them above all other people on earth. Knowing that He is a GIVING God, and that it is His will to prosper you, instead of giving in to fear, God intends you to look at your financial famine and **laugh** in the enemy's face!

God's Word is clear:

"In famine, He will redeem you from death…"

"…neither shall you be afraid of destruction when it comes. At destruction you shall laugh." (Job 5:20-22, TAB)

The reason you can laugh in the enemy's face is because you know God will not only deliver you, but He will fulfill His promises and pour His abundance into your life.

SIX MAJOR STEPS TO FINANCIAL DELIVERANCE

To experience financial deliverance and receive God' provision during your time of financial crisis, there are six major spiritual steps you must take:

1. Bind spirits of fear, worry and unbelief from your mind.

2. Get your eyes off your lack and off your financial problems.

3. Stop depending upon your own limited, natural resources and depend upon God as your Source of Total Supply.

4. Do not withhold from God your tithes and offerings. Give liberally expecting God to multiply it back into your life.

5. Line yourself up with the Word and walk in obedience to God.

6. Ask in faith, without doubting.

God's promise to you today is that in the midst of your financial needs you can come to Him and draw whatever you need from His storehouse!

God promised that in the time of famine you will be satisfied.

"The Lord knoweth the days of the upright: and their inheritance shall be for ever. They shall not be ashamed in the evil time: and in the days of famine they shall be satisfied."

Psalm 37:18-19

The word, "satisfied" in this scripture is translated from the Hebrew word, "saba" which means "to fill to satisfaction, to be full, to have plenty."

In this scripture, we are assured that God knows the ultimate destiny of those who walk uprightly before Him...their inheritance is everlasting. We know that we have an eternal inheritance waiting for us in heaven. But He is also concerned about our daily existence now, here on earth. He is concerned about your financial needs and the problems you face. He knows what you need before you ever ask! His promise to you is that in the time of adversity, you will not be put to shame. This means that whatever circumstances you face, you will never be defeated as long as you keep your faith and trust in Him.

You are neither exempt nor immune from adversity, trouble or pain; but you are promised deliverance out of all your troubles. (Proverbs 11:8) He will deliver you from the snare of the fowler! (Psalm 91:3) He will deliver you from every evil work! (2 Timothy 4:18) During times of famine, you are promised God's provision...not just enough to get by or to meet your needs but that you will have **plenty** so that you will be fully satisfied.

IT IS YOUR TIME TO BE DEBT FREE!

One of the biggest yokes of bondage in the Body of Christ today is the bondage of DEBT! Debt strangles! It kills! It holds God's people back from receiving what they need to fulfill His will in this end time hour. God promised to deliver you. You do not have to stay in financial bondage any longer!

When you face desperate financial needs, your trust must be in God's Word and the prophetic promises He has given you, not in man's limited natural resources.

Instead of trusting in man's limited resources, God wants you to act upon the Word...act upon His promises...to trust, believe and totally rely upon Him to meet all your needs.

Your trust and dependence upon God is the key to prosperity, even during times of great financial difficulty. The Word reveals that those who learn to trust...to rely totally upon God, will not be fearful or shaken when they face desperate needs or crises. Look at Jeremiah 17:8, in the Amplified Version, *"For he shall be like a tree planted by the waters, that spreads out its roots by the river; and shall not see and fear when the heat comes..."*

When you fully learn to trust God and live your life *"...not...by bread alone, but by every word that proceedeth out of the mouth of God." (Matthew 4:4)* you will never be moved! You will be like a tree that flourishes even during time of drought, *"...but his leaf shall be green; he shall not be anxious and careful in the year of drought..." (Jeremiah 17:8, TAB)*

Regardless of the financial problems and crises you face, you do not ever have to be fearful or anxious as long as you have built a solid foundation whereby your faith and trust are fixed upon God and His faithfulness to fulfill His promises. You will never suffer want but will be continually satisfied!

CAST YOUR HOOK INTO THE SEA!

Many Christians have experienced tremendous struggles, heartaches and trials in the area of their finances. There have been times when they have been so discouraged, so weary, so depressed, they did not know if they would ever survive. They were ready to give up! You may be at this point.

If you will hear the word of the Lord, believe it and act upon it in faith, God will not only release this financial anointing upon you but you will also experience the miracle of debt cancellation.

You must get your eyes off your circumstances; off the bigness of your debt and onto the supernatural provision of Almighty God! The time for you to act upon God's word to you is NOW, while this financial anointing is being released.

Jesus manifested a miracle to teach Peter not to rely upon man's resources but to draw from God's supernatural resources.

The tax collectors came to Peter to collect the yearly temple tax of a shekel which was required of every Jew. *"And when they were come to Capernaum, they that received tribute money came to Peter, and said, doth not your master pay tribute? He saith, Yes. And when he was come into the house, Jesus prevented him, saying, What thinkest thou, Simon? of whom do the kings of the earth take custom or tribute? of their own children, or of strangers? Peter saith unto him, Then are the children free. Notwithstanding, lest we should offend them, go thou to the sea, and cast an hook, and take up the fish that first cometh up; and when thou has opened his mouth, thou shalt find a piece of money: that take, and give unto them for me and thee." (Matthew 17:24-27)*

When Peter came into the house to gather the money for the taxes, Jesus stopped him. He asked Peter, "What do you think, Simon?" "From whom do the kings of the earth collect duty and taxes – from their own sons or from others?" "From others," Peter answered. Jesus said, "Then the sons are exempt."

Jesus was the Son of God. The Temple was His Father's house and He was not obligated to pay this tax for the service of the Temple. However, since He did not want to offend the Jewish leaders by refusing to pay the tax, he paid it through a miracle of debt cancellation.

Everything Jesus did was for a divine purpose. He could have had Peter pay this tax from their treasury but He did not. Instead, He chose to draw upon the supernatural resources of heaven. Jesus told Peter to go to the sea and cast his hook into the water. He told Peter to take the first fish he caught, open its mouth and he would find a piece of money in it.

Peter did not try to rationalize or determine how this could possibly take place. In the natural, it was impossible! He did not try to pump up faith to receive this miracle. He simply believed and acted according to Christ's word.

As Peter acted, God prepared a special fish with the exact amount of money in its mouth that was necessary to pay the Temple tax. Peter went to the sea and cast in his hook EXPECTING TO RECEIVE what Christ had promised.

EXPECT GOD'S SUPERNATURAL PROVISION

In the financial circumstances you face, are you looking to God EXPECTING to receive the fulfillment of His promises?

To receive a miracle of debt cancellation you must have a breakthrough that will take you beyond the limitations of your natural mind and your natural resources.

Revelation is never interpreted through the natural mind. *"But the natural man receiveth not the things of the Spirit of God: for they are foolishness unto him: neither can he know them, because they are spiritually discerned." (1 Corinthians 2:14)*

If Peter had limited what Christ could do according to his natural mind, he would never have received God's supernatural provision. It was foolish to his natural mind that a fish would have money in its mouth to pay the tax.

God wants to cancel your debt by His supernatural provision, not by the natural laws of man. If you limit what God will do for you according to your natural mind, you will never be able to comprehend how God can supernaturally cancel your debt.

Your natural mind will tell you it is impossible!

Your natural mind will tell you your debt is too large!

Your natural mind will hinder you from acting upon God's promises!

This is God's time for you to receive a miracle of debt cancellation. Act while the financial anointing is being released. Peter did not receive a miracle of debt cancellation until he cast his hook into the sea.

Right now, ask God to take you beyond the limitations of your natural mind. Ask Him to raise the level of your faith to believe and expect Him to supernaturally cancel your debt.

Cast your hook into the sea! Act upon God's promises. Give to God what He directs. Take every limitation off Him and be set free from every bondage of debt, in Jesus' Name.

SEVEN ACTION STEPS TO YOUR FINANCIAL DELIVERANCE

With your faith fixed firmly upon God's Word and knowing God will release His blessing and enable you to become debt free, you need to put your faith into action. Faith is a fact, but faith is an act!

Below are seven major practical steps you need to take:

1. Make a commitment and set a goal as to when you would like to be debt free. If you are married, you and your spouse need to both come together in agreement and make a firm commitment before God that you will do everything possible, with His help, to reduce your debts and become debt free.

2. Continue giving to God your tithe and offering even during a time of financial crisis. Withholding shuts up the windows of heaven but giving opens the windows of heaven of God's blessings. Prove God and see that He will open the windows of heaven and pour out a blessing you will not be able to contain.

3. Identify problem areas. Review your monthly expenditures to determine areas where you can cut back in spending. Make a list of areas where you agree you are spending too much money. Write down specific steps you will take and how much you will cut back.

4. Cut credit card debt. This is the first place to start reducing your debt. Stop making purchases on your credit cards. Cut up all but one of your cards and pay cash for all purchases.

5. Limit expenditures to essentials. Be disciplined and firm in establishing a strategy to not buy anything unless it is absolutely essential.

6. Develop a debt consolidation or repayment plan. Notify your creditors at the first signal that you are having a problem. Determine a reduced monthly amount you will be able to pay each creditor and get their approval. Once you have a plan, be committed and faithful to it until all your debts are repaid.

7. Consider getting a temporary job working part-time to pay off your debts.

DEBT REDUCTION STRATEGY

Once you have made a firm commitment before God to do everything within your power to become debt free, you are acting in faith upon His promises and are consistently giving your tithe and offerings, you are ready to develop a debt reduction strategy.

Do not look to the world's remedy for debt.

You cannot borrow your way out of debt! Although debt consolidation may sound good to the natural mind, it will rarely reduce the total amount of money you owe. New loan costs will be added to your balance. Consolidation borrowing almost always adds to the total debt.

The only way debt consolidation can be helpful to you is if you are able to get the interest on your total bills reduced. This will cause the debt to be paid off more quickly because more of each payment will be going toward paying off the balance of your loan. This usually only happens when a person owes large amounts of high-interest credit card debts.

God has a better answer to your debt problem. As you look to God, He will reveal specific strategies for you to implement in your war on debt and will supernaturally work on your behalf.

Don't limit God. Believe Him to help you get a raise on your job, a new job with a higher paying salary, income from unknown sources, reduced prices on a new car or house, favor with your creditors and reduced payments.

ATTACK YOUR DEBTS ONE AT A TIME

Begin your debt reduction plan by listing all your debts (excluding your house payment, rent, utilities, car payment) on the Debt Reduction Strategy form on page 122. Transfer the information from the forms in Section 3, "My Current List of Debts" (page 85) and "Credit Card Payments" (page 86).

Prioritize all your debts by listing them with the largest balances at the top and the smallest balances with the highest interest rates at the bottom.

Begin by paying off debts with the combination of highest interest rates and lowest balances. While making minimum payments on the accounts, concentrate on paying off these accounts with the small balances and highest interest rates first.

When one account is paid off, apply the amount of that payment to the next smallest account in line for elimination.

Look at the example below:

SAMPLE FAMILY DEBT REDUCTION STRATEGY

CREDITOR	BALANCE	INTEREST RATE	MINIMUM MONTHLY PAYMENT
Visa	$5,000	10.5	$100
MasterCard	$2,500	13.5	$80
Macy's	$1,500	19	$75
Student Loan	$1,000	8	$50
Finance Co.	$750	15	$35
WalMart	$500	21	$25
Penny's	$300	21	$15
Total Debt:	$11,550	Total Debt Payment: $380	

Step 1: The commitment is made to stop using credit cards, cut back on spending and to eliminate all unnecessary expenses.

Step 2: After reviewing the monthly budget and cutting back expenditures in certain categories, the sample family discover they have $150 monthly they can use in their debt reduction strategy.

Step 3: The sample family continues making the minimum monthly payments on all their accounts but concentrate on paying off the accounts with the smallest balances and highest interest rates.

Step 4: The sample family adds the $150 to their $15 payment to Penny's and in two months the bill is paid off.

Step 5: The sample family then take the $150 they were paying on their Penny's account and add it to their minimum monthly payment of $25. They start paying $175 monthly until their WalMart account is paid.

Step 6: When the WalMart account is closed, the sample family takes the $175 they were paying monthly on their WalMart account and adds it to the $35 minimum payment to the Finance Company. They start paying $210 a month until the Finance Company is paid off.

Using this debt reduction strategy, the sample family continues this process. They continue to concentrate on paying off one account at a time until all their debts are paid.

To follow this strategy, use the Debt Reduction Strategy form on page 122. As each debt is eliminated, set aside time with your family to praise God. Continue to speak and claim His promises over each debt until they are all paid. Believe God to release additional finances into your life.

TRANSFER YOUR CREDIT CARD BALANCES TO A CARD WITH THE LOWEST INTEREST RATES

This is a simple debt-reduction strategy. Check with each of the lending institutions, which have issued your credit cards. Be sure that you do the necessary research to know which card charges the lowest interest fee.

If you have an exceptionally low interest rate card, ask the lender to extend your credit limit to allow you to transfer of one, or even all your other credit card debt to it. One thing you can offer as an incentive for the lender to grant your request, is to agree to allow them to make an automatic monthly payment withdrawal from your checking account.

Once you have moved your credit card debt to the lowest possible interest rate, **do not** pay the lower minimum monthly payment which comes with your lower interest-rate-card debt. Keep your monthly payment at least as large as it was before you moved your debt.

Using this strategy, you will not only have less total debt to pay because you owe less interest, but you have a higher principal payment to pay off your debt in a shorter time period.

Once you have eliminated your debts, you will be able to set aside money you were paying toward your debts to go toward fulfilling your goals in your life plan. Keep your mission statement before you and stay focused on fulfilling God's purpose for your life.

MORTGAGE PRE-PAYMENT STRATEGIES

Can you believe God to help you pay off the mortgage to your home and save thousands of dollars in interest?

You can have a debt-free home!

But, you must raise the level of your faith and believe that it is possible and with God's help, implement strategies to accomplish this goal.

Here are several proven strategies that you can use to pay off your mortgage early:

FIRST-DAY PAYMENT STRATEGY

Find out if your present loan has any form of prepayment restriction. In many states, it is now illegal for a lender to refuse a home owner the right to prepay his mortgage.

To reap the greatest benefit from this strategy, you must make the first payment on your loan the day it is activated. In other words, the day the lender begins to charge interest on the money you are borrowing.

By doing this, a number of months will be automatically deducted from the full term of your loan. In some cases a thirty-year mortgage can be shortened by more than four years. The amount of savings fluctuates with the interest rate and terms that apply to each mortgage.

During the first years of your mortgage, only a small part of each monthly payment is applied to lowering your principal balance.

For example, with a $100,000 mortgage with an interest rate of 14.5%, if the first payment is made on the due date, only $16.23 of the $1,224.56 payment is used to pay off the balance.

One thousand two-hundred-eight dollars and thirty-three cents ($1,208.33) of that first payment goes toward interest!

However, if the first payment of $1,224.56 is made before any interest is charged, the full amount of the payment goes toward paying off the $100,000 balance.

The savings in this example will result in a deduction of four years and six months from the term of the 30-year loan. It will also result in great interest savings of $64,900.48!

This same strategy is not limited to just the first payment. It can be applied at any time during the life of your mortgage. However, it accomplishes the greatest results with the first payment.

If three payments of $1224.56 ($3,673.68) are made when the loan closes and before the interest is due, there would be a savings of $104,061.69 in interest and seven years and three months would be saved!

SPLIT-PAYMENT STRATEGY

Another strategy for rapid mortgage reduction is to make a half payment every two weeks (fourteen days). This plan will cause you to automatically make one extra payment every year. You will also lower the principle balance of your loan twenty-six times instead of 12 times per year.

There are fifty-two weeks in each year. If a half payment is made every two weeks, you will make twenty-six payments each year. Twenty-six half payments are equal to thirteen whole payments. If you only make one full payment each month you will make twelve payments each year.

Using this split-payment strategy, you will be making a paydown on the balance of your note every fourteen days. This means you will be paying interest on a rapidly decreasing principal amount.

Using the example of a thirty-year mortgage of $100,000 at 7% interest, if this mortgage is paid with the split-payment strategy, it will save $34,464.25 and reduce the amount of time to pay off this mortgage by six years and three months.

This strategy can be applied to your mortgage, even it is not a new one.

PRINCIPAL-REDUCTION STRATEGY

This strategy is very flexible because you determine the amount you want to pay above your regular payment. It can be a one-time payment, a monthly payment, an annual payment or any combination of these.

You may desire to pay down $100 each month beyond your regular payment or make two extra payments per year. On a thirty-year mortgage of $100,000 at 8% interest, paying an extra $100 each month above your regular payment you would be able to save $62,460.31 and reduce the amount of time to pay off the loan by nine years and ten months.

PLANNED-INCREASE PAYMENT STRATEGY

This strategy requires a lot of discipline to plan for a systematic percentage of increase in your house payment each year.

To implement this strategy, you must increase your monthly payment by one percent each year, beginning with the first payment through the first twelve months. Then you must increase the payment by one percent each year thereafter. Each year you should plan your budget to allow you to add one percent to the previous year's payment. (You can increase the payment by any percentage you desire but just make sure your budget can handle it.)

Using the example of increasing your payment one percent each year, a thirty-year, $100,000 mortgage at 14.5% interest, will be paid off in its entirety in only twelve years and at a savings in interest of $151,778.84!

These strategies are just a few of the many you can implement to pay off your mortgage early and save thousands of dollars in interest.

Each individual's financial situation and indebtedness is different. You must look carefully at all the options available to you, seek God's guidance and trust Him to enable you to develop your debt-reduction plan that will enable you to be debt free.

DECLARATION OF FAITH TO BECOME DEBT FREE

I hereby make a commitment before God that I will take control of my finances and discipline myself and my family to do everything within our power to become debt free.

- We commit and consecrate our finances to God. We will put God first in our finances and everything we do.

- We take God at His promise that He will throw back the floodgates of Heaven and pour out His blessings in such proportion we will not be able to contain it.

- We believe God will rebuke the power of the enemy and break the bondage of debt from our lives.

- We bind spirits of fear, worry and unbelief concerning our finances from our minds.

- We will take our eyes off our lack and off our financial problems and will keep them focused upon God and His power to deliver us.

- We will no longer depend upon our own limited, natural resources but will depend upon God as our Source of total supply.

- We will not withhold from God our tithes and offerings, but will give willingly, liberally, expecting God to multiply it back into our lives. Start now with a special gift to MCWE to win souls!

- We will line ourselves up with God's Word and walk in obedience to Him.

- We will come before God concerning our needs and ask in faith without doubting.

- We are believing God to release His supernatural provision into our lives. And, as we act in faith according to His promises, we believe we will be able to pay all our debts and receive His blessings to live in a cycle of His supernatural provision.

Signed this day _____

_____   _____
Signature   Signature

_____   _____
Signature   Signature

_____   _____
Signature (Morris Cerullo)   Signature (Theresa Cerullo)

(Note: Ask each member of your family to sign this faith declaration. Send it to me and Theresa to sign and anoint with oil. We will agree with you concerning God's promise to deliver you from financial bondage and help you to become debt free. We will send it back to you.)

"Again I say unto you, That if two of you shall agree on earth as touching any thing that they shall ask, it shall be done for them of my Father which is in heaven."   *Matthew 18:19*

Note: It is extremely important for you to fill out and sign this declaration NOW. Tear it off and mail it to:

Morris Cerullo World Evangelism
U.S.: P.O. Box 85277 • San Diego, CA 92186-5277
Canada: P.O. Box 3600 • Concord, Ontario L4k 1b6
U.K.:P.O. Box 277 • Hemel Hempstead, HERTS HP2 7dh

CLIP AND MAIL

DEBT REDUCTION STRATEGY

WORKSHEET

CREDITOR	BALANCE	INTEREST RATE	MINIMUM MONTHLY PAYMENT
Total Debt:			**Total Debt Payment:**
$			$

I am sowing now according to my need $_____ for my Debt Cancellation Miracle from God.

_____   _____

Signature   Date

DEVELOP A DEBT ELIMINATION PLAN

The Cycle of Financial Defeat

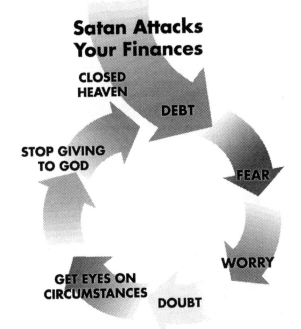

Satan Attacks Your Finances

CLOSED HEAVEN

DEBT

STOP GIVING TO GOD

FEAR

GET EYES ON CIRCUMSTANCES

DOUBT

WORRY

God will help you break the cycle of financial defeat. Those who give liberally will receive an increase and will prosper. The Apostle Paul said that those who give liberally shall reap abundance but those who give sparingly will reap a small harvest. (2 Corinthians 9:6)

To break the bondage of poverty and debt from your life, you must determine in your heart that you will not withhold from giving to God but will continue to sow seed...to give liberally and faithfully your tithes and special offerings as He directs you.

SECTION 6

RETIREMENT AND ESTATE PLANNING

A good man leaves an inheritance for his children's children, but a sinner's wealth is stored up for the righteous.

Proverbs 13:22, (NIV)

SECTION 6

RETIREMENT AND ESTATE PLANNING

As you develop a Life/Financial plan, you need to include strategies to reach your savings goals. In chapter two, "Focus On Your God-given Vision," you identified the vision and purpose God has for your life as well as specific goals in fulfilling your purpose. You determined the total costs for the fulfillment of your goals and the amount of monthly savings you will need for ministry, personal growth and retirement goals.

As your debts are paid off, it will free more money for you to set aside as savings toward the fulfillment of these goals.

One of the most common mistakes people make in their financial planning is not having specific savings and investment goals. As a steward of God's finances, ask Him to direct you. *"Trust in the Lord with all your heart and lean not on your own understanding; in all your ways acknowledge him, and he will make your paths straight." (Proverbs 3:5-6)*

You may think, "I have so little money to save that it won't make any difference." Or, you may think you are so far in debt that you don't have any money to put in savings or investments.

The sooner you start planning and saving, the sooner you will be able to benefit. Look at the table below. It illustrates the potential increase for just two dollars deposited monthly.

$$$$$$$ SAVINGS $$$$$$$				
This table shows what $2 deposited monthly will grow to in different time periods under various interest rates.				
What $2 Deposited Monthly Will Grow To				
Years	Rate 3%	6%	9%	12%
1	24.72	25.44	26.16	26.88
3	76.40	81.00	85.76	90.70
5	131.24	143.40	156.56	170.76
10	283.38	335.32	397.44	471.72
15	459.76	592.14	768.08	1,002.08
20	664.24	935.82	1,338.34	1,936.76
25	901.28	1,395.76	2,215.78	3,584.02

If you do not already have a savings plan, start today. Some financial planners advise a person to allocate 5% of their monthly income for savings. You may want to set aside more or less, depending upon your current financial situation. The important thing is that you save on a consistent basis.

Let me give you another example. Look at the table below. This chart illustrates the cost in delaying investing. For example, if a couple at the age of 25 makes a commitment to invest $2000 per year until they reach the age of 65. With an average rate of return of 8% over that period they will have accumulated $606,487. However, if for some reason they waited until the age of 35 to start saving, they will have only $266.427 at age 65. The cost for their delay: $340,060.

Investment Started at age:	Average Rate of Return	Cash Value of Investment At Age 65
25	8%	$606,487
35	8%	$266,427
45	8%	$108,914
55	8%	$ 35,954

It is especially important to begin saving early in life and planning for your retirement. However, research indicates that 39% of U. S. households have no retirement savings at all. One of the many reasons great majorities of people do not have savings for their retirement is due to the current economic pressures. Retirement savings are often considered an extra rather than a necessity. It is often the last consideration after all the other financial goals have been achieved.

The best time to start saving for your retirement is as early as your mid-20's. However, you can still accumulate $250,000 in a tax-deferred account by age 65 if you start investing at ages 40, 45 or 50. Look at the table below. Even if you not have been able to save towards your retirement until later in life, it is never too late to start.

RETIREMENT SAVINGS POSSIBILITIES			
Monthly Savings Required At Various Rates of Earnings			
Investment Started At Age: 3%	6%	9%	12%
40 $571	$380	$246	$157
45 $775	$566	$407	$289
50 $1,120	$895	$710	$559

RETIREMENT BUDGET

As you plan for your retirement, the first thing you need to do is to develop a retirement budget. Determine what your retirement income will be and compare it with your monthly expenses to see what you can expect. Your retirement income may include income from different sources such as: Social Security, employer pensions, profit-sharing plans, thrift plans, 401 (k)s, 403 (b)s, employment deferred compensation, IRA's, savings, investments and inheritances.

Use the form on page 136 to determine your projected Retirement Income. As you review your total source of retirement income, ask yourself the following questions:

a. Will I have sufficient funds to cover my budgeted expenses?

b. Will it be necessary for me to cut back my living expenses?

c. What will be the best time to retire?

d. Should I consider part-time employment?

e. How much extra income do I need and how much money do I need to save monthly to meet my financial goals for retirement

DETERMINE YOUR RETIREMENT GOALS

What are your plans for the future? Would you like to retire at age 62 on 80% of your income? Or, would you like to continue working as long as possible, while storing money away? It is very important to make your goals as specific as possible. Both spouses should set aside time to pray together, discuss and agree upon their retirement goals.

As you reach retirement age, one of your major goals should be to be debt free with the majority of your needed funds in high-yielding investments.

The most flexible retirement accounts are individual retirement accounts (IRAs). IRAs are not investments themselves. They are retirement accounts that shelter income by delaying the income taxes until the funds are withdrawn. As you age, your tax rate decreases and IRAs allow you to pay less tax on your investments.

It is an excellent goal to have your home paid for before you retire, especially if you will have a limited retirement income. If you have lived in your home for at least 2 years, you may decide to sell it, using the capital gains exclusion (for people 55 or over), downsize to a smaller home or condominium and invest the tax-free profit for retirement income.

PREPARING YOUR WILL

Being a good steward of all that God has given you not only involves financial planning for your finances while you are living but also financial planning of your estate after your death. You will want to minimize taxes and preserve your estate for your family and the Lord's work.

With smart planning not only can you protect the assets you wish to leave your heirs, you can give thousands of dollars more to the Lord's work than you could without a plan.

Don't put off your estate planning to wait for a more convenient time. That time will never come.

One of the most important steps to take in planning your estate is to prepare a will. If you die without leaving a will, you will leave the door open for the state government to decide what will happen to your possessions.

Your estate includes your house, car(s), furniture, electronic equipment, antiques, books, retirement benefits, investments, life insurance and savings.

Many – often the young, or those who feel that their estate is small – believe that a will represents an unnecessary expense. But the preparation of a will should not be expensive.

Even when property distribution issues are not numerous, the will is the legal avenue through which a number of issues should be addressed:

- Naming an executor

- Avoiding the expense of a Bond

- Naming a legal guardian for minors

- Making gifts or transfers

- Reducing estate tax liability

A WILL ENABLES YOU TO DETERMINE THE DISTRIBUTION OF YOUR ASSETS

Without a will state law determines what becomes of your assets. The court has guidelines for distributing property that must be followed regardless of special circumstances.

For example, the law may require that all assets be distributed equally among all your children. However, what if you have a child with special problems? A will enables you to specifically state how you wish to continue providing for your family.

A WILL ENABLES YOU TO MAKE SPECIAL BEQUESTS

In addition to family members, you may have friends and other loved ones to whom you wish to leave assets. If you have a special heirloom that has always been admired by your close friend, you can make this bequest in your will and know that your friend will receive the heirloom as a warm remembrance.

You can even designate a memorial gift to your favorite charity. This allows you to pay special tribute to a loved one while also perpetuating your personal dedication to our ministry.

A WILL ENABLES YOU TO NAME A PERSONAL REPRESENTATIVE

Without a will, the court will name an administrator to settle your estate. The court appointed administrator may not be the person you would have chosen for this important function. However, with a will, you can name a particular individual or financial institution as personal representative of your estate.

You may also find it helpful to name an alternative personal representative in case the first person you name is unable to serve.

A WILL ENABLES YOU TO INCLUDE MORRIS CERULLO WORLD EVANGELISM

Your support means a great deal to our ministry. A bequest can be a specific dollar amount, a fixed percentage of your estate, or it can state that Morris Cerullo World Evangelism receive the residue of the estate after provisions for all other beneficiaries have been made.

A WILL CAN SAVE YOU MONEY

A well drafted will can help you eliminate any unnecessary expenses in settling your estate.

For example, by providing a clause in your will, you can free your heirs from certain costs, such as a bond fee and other administrative charges. In addition, if you leave a bequest to Morris Cerullo World Evangelism, it will be exempt from any federal estate, state inheritance or death taxes.

A WILL ENABLES YOU TO ESTABLISH A TRUST TO PROVIDE INCOME FOR ANOTHER PERSON

By creating a testamentary trust, you are able to guarantee income for someone who may not be capable of managing a large sum of money. Income from this type of trust can support someone for life and the remainder of the trust can be distributed after that person's life.

The remainder could be donated to Morris Cerullo World Evangelism for the benefit of training Nationals and saving souls.

A WILL GIVES YOU FLEXIBILITY TO ADJUST YOUR WISHES AS CHANGE OCCURS

Family circumstances change…for example, you may have additional children or grandchildren. Or, you may have recently acquired assets such as real estate or securities that need to be included in the assets you are distributing in your will.

These are just a few of the possible changes that can affect the distribution of your assets as outlined in your will. Any changes concerning distribution of your assets can be handled through a codicil to your will.

THE BEQUEST

The charitable bequest affords a way for virtually anyone to express specific charitable wishes. In fact, the bequest is the most frequently utilized method for support of charities in America.

A bequest may take on a number of forms, including:
- A specific dollar amount
- A percentage of the estate's residual value
- A specific asset

The charitable spirit is given a voice when wishes are expressed in the will. While many may think charitable giving is reserved for a few, the truth is that every bequest to Morris Cerullo World Evangelism makes a mark that will last throughout eternity.

If you would like more information on wills and a free guide for making a Christian will, which includes sample language for making a charitable donation, we invite you to fill out the form on page139, detach it and mail it to:

Mr. Roger Artz
Sr. Vice President of Development
Morris Cerullo Development Department
P. O. Box 85277
San Diego, CA 92186-5277
Telephone: 858-277-2200, ext. 2233
Fax (858) 614-1915
e-mail: development@mcwe.com

CHARITABLE GIFT ANNUITY PLAN

For an annuity of $1,000, or more, to Morris Cerullo World Evangelism, you receive a lifetime income at a fixed rate based on your age. When your gift annuity is issued, your rate of return will never change. Additional annuities purchased over the years may **pay higher rates** because you will be older. Survivor annuities are also available (rates are slightly lower).

- **Financial Security**

  We know that you want to be sure this plan is sound. Morris Cerullo World Evangelism Gift annuities are solid. The annuities are regulated and monitored by the California State Insurance commissioner and backed by all of Morris Cerullo World Evangelism's assets to **guarantee payments** to you for life.

- **Two Benefits**

  Immediately, you are reaping a **double benefit:** regular payments for yourself and a greater outreach for souls around the world.

- **A Third Benefit**

  Since only a portion of the funds you place with Morris Cerullo World Evangelism is used to provide your annuity payment, the Internal Revenue Service has ruled that the remainder is considered a **tax deductible** contribution. In addition, a part of the payment you receive is exempt from federal income tax for your life expectancy. For each annuity, you will receive an annual tax information sheet to aid in filling out your federal income tax return.

- **Other Benefits**

  Here are other benefits you may want to consider when funding a Charitable Gift Annuity:

  By funding your annuity with appreciated securities, you receive additional tax benefits. Only a portion of the capital gain is taxable, and it would be reported each year over your life expectancy.

  You may want to consider a Deferred Payment Gift Annuity. For a gift of $1,000, or more, you can receive a charitable deduction now, but defer your Gift Annuity payments to a later date. By deferring your payments, your rate of return will be higher.

  A Deferred Payment Gift Annuity is for younger people and those who have adequate income and would rather receive their payments when they are in a lower tax bracket. (Please write for more information)

If you have been looking for a way to make a commitment to the work of the Lord while assuring yourself a lifetime income, this Charitable Gift Annuity can help you achieve both goals. When you make your gift for an Annuity, it cannot be altered.

(For specific legal advice, your should contact your own attorney)

- **Your Annuity Benefit**

To determine your annual income, use the gift annuity rate table on the back of the application and follow these steps:

1. Decide on the amount of your gift. ($1,000 minimum)

2. Determine your age at nearest birthday. (If it is less than six months until your next birthday, you are considered the age you will be on that birthday)

3. Find the rate of payment for your nearest age.

4. Multiply your gift annuity by this rate to determine your annual income. This income will be sent to you in equal quarterly payments.

- **How To Apply**

1. Complete the application form on page 137. Please include all information requested and sign on the space provided. Clip and mail today.

2. Make your check ($1,000 minimum) payable to: Morris Cerullo World Evangelism.

3. Mail application and check to:

Morris Cerullo World Evangelism
Deferred Giving Department
P. O. Box 85277
San Diego, CA 92186-5277
Tel. (858) 277-2200; Fax (858) 614-1915
e-mail: development@mcwe.com

RETIREMENT AND ESTATE PLANNING

RETIREMENT INCOME WORKSHEET

Sources of regular income	$ _____
Social security benefits	$ _____
Pensions	$ _____
Annuities	$ _____
Other	$ _____
Total Monthly Regular Income	$ _____
Retirement assets held in tax-deferred accounts	$ _____
Individual retirement accounts	$ _____
Keogh plans	$ _____
401(k), 403(b) or 457 plans	$ _____
Tax sheltered annuities	$ _____
Other	$ _____
Total Assets Held in Tax-Deferred Accounts	$ _____
Other Assets Available for Retirement	$ _____
Money-market funds	$ _____
Certificates of deposit	$ _____
Treasury bills	$ _____
Common stocks	$ _____
Bonds	$ _____
Mutual funds	$ _____
Real estate investments	$ _____
Business interests	$ _____
Other	$ _____
Total Other Assets	$ _____
1. Total Monthly Regular Income	$ _____
2. Total Assets Held In Tax-Deferred Accounts	$ _____
3. Total Other Assets	$ _____
Total Value of all Assets for Retirement Income	$ _____

RETIREMENT AND ESTATE PLANNING

APPLICATION FOR GIFT ANNUITY CERTIFICATE

I hereby apply for a Gift Annuity Certificate to be used under the Morris Cerullo World Evangelism Gift Annuity Plan and enclose my payment for that purpose in the amount of $_____ . I understand that of this amount, part will represent a gift and part will be used to purchase a life annuity contract for my benefit in accordance with the gift annuity rates established by committee on gift annuities at the time of my application set forth on page 138. I understand further that this amount is not subject to withdrawal and that no portion of it shall be refundable.

❑ Mr. ❑ Mrs. ❑ Miss

_____ Birth Date _____
First Annuitant   M/D/Y

_____ Telephone (   )_____
Street Address

_____ _____
City   State   Zip   Social Security Number

For a Survivor Life Annuity, use this space for the Second Annuitant. (The Two-life Annuity rate is lower than the Single-life Annuity rate and will be quoted upon request).

❑ Mr. ❑ Mrs. ❑ Miss

_____ Birth Date _____
First Annuitant   M/D/Y

_____ Telephone (   )_____
Street Address

_____ _____
City   State   Zip   Social Security Number

I understand that payments will be made quarterly and will terminate at the death of the Applicant if a Single-life Annuity is desired, or at the death of the Survivor if a Two-life Annuity is desired.

Applicant's or Donor's Signature _____ Date _____

Donor's Address (If other than Applicant)_____

City_____State _____ Date _____

Make checks payable to: **Morris Cerullo World Evangelism Deferred Giving Department • P. O. Box 85277 • San Diego, CA 92186-5277 • Tel. (858) 277-2200; Fax (858) 614-1915 e-mail: development@mcwe.com**

SECTION 6

RETIREMENT AND ESTATE PLANNING

GIFT ANNUITY RATES

Approximate Values One Life   (The rates are subject to change with change in interest rates.)

AGE	PAYOUT RATE	GIFT AMOUNT	INCOME	TAXED RETURN OF PRINCIPAL
60	6.4%	0.29	54.1%	45.9%
65	6.7%	0.33	50.1%	49.9%
70	7.2%	0.37	45.4%	54.6%
72	7.4%	0.40	43.6%	56.4%
74	7.7%	0.41	41.6%	58.4%
76	8.0%	0.43	39.6%	60.4%
78	8.4%	0.45	37.1%	62.9%
80	8.9%	0.46	35.5%	64.5%
82	9.4%	0.48	33.2%	66.8%
84	10.1%	0.49	30.9%	69.1%
86	10.8%	0.51	28.8%	71.2%
88	11.4%	0.53	26.9%	73.1%
90	12.0%	0.56	25.2%	74.8%

ACGA Rates Effective 7-1-01

Approximate Values Two Lives

AGE		PAYOUT RATE	GIFT AMOUNT	INCOME	TAXED RETURN OF PRINCIPAL
60	55	5.8%	0.22	58.1%	41.9%
65	60	6.2%	0.22	54.4%	45.6%
70	65	6.4%	0.27	50.3%	49.7%
72	67	6.5%	0.29	48.4%	51.6%
74	69	6.7%	0.30	46.6%	53.4%
76	71	6.8%	0.33	44.8%	55.2%
78	73	7.0%	0.35	42.8%	57.2%
80	75	7.3%	0.36	40.9%	59.1%
82	77	7.5%	0.39	38.6%	61.4%
84	79	7.9%	0.40	36.4%	63.6%
86	81	8.3%	0.42	34.8%	65.2%
88	83	8.7%	0.44	32.7%	67.3%
90	85	9.2%	0.46	30.6%	69.4%

RETIREMENT AND ESTATE PLANNING

REQUEST FOR MORE INFORMATION ON PREPARING MY WILL

❏ Please send me more information on wills and a free guide for making a Christian will.

❏ I would like to receive sample information for including a charitable donation in my will.

❏ I am considering including Morris Cerullo World Evangelism in my will.

❏ I have real estate or stock I can give.

Name_____

Address_____

City_____ State _____ Zip _____

Telephone ( ) _____ E-Mail _____

Fill out this form, clip and mail to:

Morris Cerullo Development Department

P. O. Box 85277

San Diego, CA 92186-5277

Telephone: 858-277-2200, ext. 2233

Fax (858) 614-1915

e-mail: development@mcwe.com